WRITING THE FUTURE

English and the making of a culture of innovation

Gunther Kress

NATE
PAPERS IN EDUCATION

Writing the Future is published by the National Association for the Teaching of English (NATE), the UK subject teacher association for all aspects of the teaching of English from pre-school to university.

NATE
50 Broadfield Road
Broadfield Business Centre
Sheffield S8 0XJ
Tel: 0 114 255 5419
Fax: 0 114 255 5296

Distributed exclusively in the United States of America by
National Council of Teachers of English
1111 W. Kenyon Road, Urbana, Illinois 61801-1096

Published by arrangement with NATE.

ISBN 0 901291 43 9

NCTE Stock Number: 58951

First published 1995

Cover design by Barry Perks Graphic Design

For Jill
Who is there, always.

The author

Gunther Kress is Professor of Education (with special reference to the teaching of English) at the Institute of Education, University of London.

Contents

Preface

One of the lasting achievements of Conservative governments in the 1980s, whether here in the UK, in the US, or in Australia, has been to show, decisively, that education is a political matter. This wasn't a polite thing to say before – even though it was a truth commonly understood. Anyone interested in social as in economic futures now understands that the education system is a central component of that infrastructure which supports economic life – along with transport, telecommunications, the financial system, and so on. That makes it right and proper that governments take an active interest; and it makes it right and proper and essential that all of the rest of us – parents, teachers, administrators, academics, business men and women, take an active interest. We all have a say.

If we all have a say, as we *must*, that makes education a political matter which goes beyond party-politics. It affects us all; it shapes *all* our futures: the well-being of children now in schools depends on the building of social and economic futures which do offer a *real* stake, to *all*, in that future. For a post-imperial, post-industrial society such as that of Britain, the possibility of productive futures rests, absolutely, on the building of a culture of innovation, in all domains: in the field of social thinking – is it conceivable that we will enter the twenty-first century as we leave the twentieth, with theories and nostrums about work, and leisure, fulfilment, social purposes, equity, which were developed pretty well two hundred years ago, when Britain led the world from the era of agrarian feudalism into the world of industrialism? Similarly in the fields of economic theory, of culture, politics: how do we rethink the idea of the nation-state (we now have a *National* Curriculum) in the era of radical globalisation of finance, transport, culture, communication, the media, and production.

Innovation is not a neutral concept. All sorts of things can be innovated, as Europe has learned bitterly during this century. Creativity is not neutral; creative accounting is not an unproblematic good. Nevertheless, a culture founded on innovation as a taken-for-granted characteristic will, simply, be essential to any hope of productive futures. That leaves the debate over what the directions and contents of innovation should be to another occasion. The alternative is a culture of conservatism and reaction: it is not one which looks promising. The histories of Spain and Portugal after their loss of empire stand as a warning of one possible future for Britain.

Innovation is something you work for; it cannot be wished, and it cannot be legislated. Nor can it happen in one area alone; it has to be an activity worked for across all cultural, economic, technological, political and social domains. You can't pursue a scorched-earth policy in relation to the Arts and the Humanities, and hope for real innovation in technology. Humans, alas and thankfully, and human societies, work in much more subtle and complex ways than that.

It is that realisation which puts English at the very centre, absolutely, of any attempts at remaking present paths into the future. For me, two major considerations stand out: English is a vastly complex subject, more than any other in the English school system. It is, above all, the subject which deals with the means of representation and communication: the means whereby we say who we are, to ourselves and to others; the means whereby we can examine the visions others before us have had about themselves and their times; and the means of giving voice to our visions, for ourselves, and for others: the proposal of alternatives for debate, and, after that debate, for common action.

The second foundational consideration concerns the function of the curriculum: a curriculum is, always, a design for the future. In the knowledges, practices, values which it puts forward – and in their modes of transmission in pedagogies – it imagines a certain kind of human being, with particular characteristics. If I teach grammar as a set of rules which must be observed absolutely, I engender, in the young human who accepts this, a particular attitude to authority and therefore a particular notion of who she or he is or can be. The young person who rejects this view is still affected: their view will be that of a rejection of authority. If I teach grammar as a resource, which is constantly newly made by those who use it in the course of their lives, out of *their interests*, I engender a potentially quite different notion of that person about himself or herself, and about their place in society.

As the curriculum of the means of representation, of communication, of values, English has an absolutely central role in this process. I am certain that Science and Mathematics have a similar role: they too propose particular modes of seeing and being. What English does, which the others cannot, is to make such issues into the subject of debate, critique, and evaluation.

It has been put to me that the proposals in this book are too optimistic, and ignore the greater and more likely realities of a starkly bleak future – of social disintegration, of unemployment, of despair. I have never regarded myself as belonging to the Pollyanna tendency of social speculation. It is my simple conviction that we are, at the moment, at a point where a choice can still be made; and I feel it therefore as my responsibility, absolutely, to act in such ways as I can, where and when I can, to bring about a different future. Neal Acherson in a recent piece in *The Independent* quotes Pastor Niemöller: it is no good getting on the wrong train, and then, once inside, running in the opposite direction to where it's going, shouting that you didn't want to go that way at all.

That has been the traditional role of the academic: to offer critique of actions set in train by others. My view is that our present is a time when critique is no longer enough, and in fact is no longer the real issue: the real issue is that of the proposal of alternative visions; reviving that unfashionable genre of the Utopia, and acting strongly in contesting, in public life, alternatives which do not offer the values that I, you, we, believe should shape our tomorrow.

That has led me to act as I have done over the last few years, quite unlike anything I used to think academics should do, and it has led me to write this small volume.

What do I hope to achieve? Sir Ron Dearing's five-year moratorium on curriculum changes in England, has provided – not so much a breathing space – but a space for starting a fundamental debate about the shape of the future and the essential role of English in that. This book is offered as a means of starting a debate: not as a contribution to establishing new givens. My hope is for an intense debate over two, three years, out of which can come not necessarily agreement, but *understanding*, understanding of a new agenda. Out of that agenda all of us involved in teaching English can then begin to make the outline of a curriculum which will do the job that we think it should.

At the end of that period of five or six years the profession can then be in a position to take the lead, together with parents, and politicians, people in business and industry, in making new proposals for an English curriculum that plays a central part in the making of a productive, a working future.

A note on 'culturalisms'

Words are constantly fought over. To use a word is to take sides, wittingly or not. When I came here some three years ago I used the term 'multicultural' to describe a situation common to both Australia and Britain. Little did I know that that word had become problematic here. So throughout this book I use a number of terms – partly to signal that this is a complex field, and contested, and partly because each term offers a different 'take' on the issues.

Throughout the book I use the word *England*. I use it to mean England – that is, a political entity not including Wales, or Scotland, or Northern Ireland. I sometimes use Britain, for that larger area. I know very little about Wales or Scotland *and*, given my life of moving between the northern and southern hemispheres, I hope that readers outside England will understand that this is an attempt to acknowledge the real historical, social, and cultural characteristics of their place. It is not an attempt to slight.

Ideas, like all the products of human work, rest on the work of many. For me, the ideas in this book come out of an experience of spending significant chunks of my life in quite different places, geographically, socially, and culturally. Having left school at the age of fourteen to become an apprentice in one place, then continuing to work in 'my trade' in a very different place, I use the word work to mean work, whether manual or intellectual; and I see little difference between them, at one level. Having lived in three very different cultures, with their achievements, their difficulties, *culture* is, for me, a big issue – as are ways of making meaning. But always, ideas come from interaction with others: social practice throws up problems, in talking and reading we find ways of dealing with these problems, of making our sense out of them. Out of all of that comes that seemingly abstract thing: 'Theory'.

I have learned from very many people. And while it is invidious not to mention all, it seems necessary to mention some. My working and talking, over many years, with David Aers, Tony Trew and Bob Hodge, with Jim Martin, Mary Macken, with Terry Threadgold, Mary Kalantzis, Bill Cope, Theo van Leeuwen, with Arnie Goldman; more recently, here in London, with Ken Jones and Mary Scott; with Michael Young, Euan Reid, Roger Hewitt, Jill Bourne, Jon Ogborn, Bob Ferguson, John Hardcastle; conversations with new friends in the US and in Germany, learning new concerns and new ways of seeing, with Jim Gee, Ben

Bachmair, Ingrid Gogolin. All of that is, in some way, in here – even though none of those named might either recognise or approve of any of it. The people who come from all over the world to study at the Institute of Education bring the richest mix of experiences – and of challenges to anyone's thinking. They make it impossible, rightly, to think in local terms.

But above all, I wish to thank another group of people here – English teachers, advisers, inspectors, who have invited me to workshops and conferences, and whose ideas and support made me feel that there was something here to carry on with. Again the names are too many to mention, so a few will have to signify my debt to all: Dave Allen, Janet White, Peter Martin, Shona Walton, Alastair West, Margaret Cooke, Andrew Burns. Anne Barnes' encouragement gave me the confidence to write this small book; Angel Scott's enthusiasm and work has carried it forward. Lesley Aers spoke to me about issues of classrooms, English, politics of curriculum, when these all were strange ideas and foreign places to me, way back then in the early 1970s, in Norwich. Those conversations started a long train of thought: and so I think that, really, she is to blame.

And then, when all this has been said, this little book would not exist without the work – generously given – of preparing the typescript in the hurly-burly of a demanding job. And for that I wish to thank Judy Benstead.

Gunther Kress
London, April 1995

I wish to express my thanks to the National Association of Advisers in English, who invited me to give a talk on the issues raised in this book to their annual conference, in Durham, January 1993.

Introduction

Futures out of our present past: escaping nostalgias

My aim in writing this little book is to issue an invitation to participate in a debate focused on the part which the English curriculum can, should and must play in the making of social futures. It offers some initial thoughts on the outlines around and along which that debate might develop. It offers no specific description of a curriculum, no pedagogy, nothing on particular forms of assessment. On the other hand everything said here is meant to bear directly on all those matters.

The present is a time of the profoundest, epochal change. I hesitated before writing that: overstatement can so easily weaken a case. I do think it is appropriate. The certainties which formed the life of my generation, and of the generation before, are unravelling, or are being unmade: the certainties of the nation-state; of the achievements of three centuries of the European project of the Enlightenment – though it is essential to bear in mind that this is also a global phenomenon, even though I see it from my Western perspective; of modernism – which saw the holocaust, but which also saw, in Europe, the humane achievements of the elimination of starvation through poverty; death through absence of health-care provisions; saw a certain minimal dignity guaranteed for everyone's old age through state provision; saw jobs that lasted for a working lifetime. The older two of my children, who are in their mid-twenties, already live in the new common-sense in which none of these are taken for granted – even though their education through school and through university prepared them for a future modelled on what was then already the past.

And still, all this might not deserve the adjective 'epochal'. I see the present, however, as the culmination of a period not of the last two or three hundred years, a span of between seven and ten 'generations', but as the culmination of an era that has lasted over seven, eight hundred years. Imagine a painting by Pieter Breughel the younger – *The Wedding Feast* perhaps. It is a scene which, in many ways, recalls my childhood in a village in Franconia; it is a scene familiar from the early episodes of Edgar Reisz' *Heimat*; and it is a scene familiar from sepia-toned photographs of the interwar years in Britain: a mode of life in which agriculture dominates, even if, during the last hundred years, that was already a myth existing only in popular conception; in which the motive-power is that of animals: the horse in agriculturally advanced countries such as England; the ox in other parts (the cow in the case of my Franconian village!); wood is the dominant material for the making of implements; food is plain for most, except on feast-days; and so on. It is a scene which could still be found in parts of Southern Europe in the mid-1970s, and which has now gone from Europe everywhere and absolutely.

It is my contention that it is this change, subtending the in-themselves enormous contemporary changes, unrecognised and therefore untreatable, that has given rise to the massive nostalgias of the later 1980s and the 1990s. The metaphors which, invisibly and potently, ruled, guided, shaped, our ordinary everyday lives, quite simply no longer work, and no amount of mythologising effort ('old ladies on bicycles', 'warm beer', 'languid, cricket-punctuated afternoons') can restore them. We live at the precise point in which the era which shaped Europe for eight hundred years has come to its end. The effects of revolution in industry, in transport, of the economy, of social structures, which date back, in the case of Britain, to the mid-eighteenth century, overlaid by intense technological advances over the last three decades have suddenly, like the flood-waters backing up behind a flimsy dam, overwhelmed the mythic structures of our consciousness in a change so rapid and far-reaching that we do not seem to have the means of coping.

In this context it is crucial to ask the most searching questions about curricula, and about English in particular. Curricula attempt to prepare young people for their society. Even a generously searching reading of the National Curriculum in English will not find much that goes beyond present understandings of the present. Given the psychological and social pressures produced by the (unrecognised causes of) current nostalgias, there are changes, all too apparent, for the curriculum, of two kinds: on the one hand, an authoritarianism engendered out of a lack of understanding of present changes, cloaked in nostalgias of various kinds, and therefore backward-looking; and on the other hand, a pragmatism and utilitarianism about the aims of (English) Education, engendered out of an equal uncertainty, but cloaked this time in 'hard-nosed' practicalities, in particular the needs and aims as they are assumed to exist in business, industry, commerce.

Neither of these is likely to produce a conception of the curriculum which will fulfil its task of contributing in a foundational sense to the making of a culture of innovation. To do that we need to focus, with as much clarity and wit as we can, on the outlines of the characteristics of the future. And we need to see the English curriculum *not only* in its traditional role of *preparing students for* that future, but to see the curriculum, and the people who experience it, *as making and shaping* that future through their competent and confident action.

To state some of my own principles quite early on: I am firmly of the opinion that everything in the new curriculum will need to be judged in terms of its effect in giving young people certain dispositions: confident in the face of difference – cultural, linguistic, ethnic, ethical – and confident in the everyday experience of change; able to see change and difference as entirely usual conditions of cultural and social life; *and* to see them as essential productive resources. My own aim is to move away from a conception of the critical reader, beholder, or commentator – away that is, from a position of *insight* which provides the ability to produce analytic critique, as the central goal of a humanistic education. Critique is an essential element of informed citizenship, and of public participation; in my envisaged future society it will be seen as an essential component in producing the new goal of *education as social action: the envisaging, design, and making of alternatives*. This ability, it seems to me, will be central to the felicitous progress of so-called post-industrial societies.

This brings me to the central principle: the social human whom I envisage through this curriculum will have been given the means of making lives which are fulfilling, have dignity, and are capable of producing happiness. These things – as the famous Monty Python sketch demonstrated ('eh you were lucky, you had a shoebox; we only had a hole in t' ground') – are historically contingent, relative. The world of tomorrow may offer its inhabitants a lesser level of material well-being, *and yet* an at least equal and perhaps greater level of satisfaction.

English is central in this task. No other subject in the curriculum has that potential, or that task; nor can I see that changing in the short-term, say over the next ten to fifteen years. It assumes some deep transformations in the subject English – in the context of a multicultural, multilingual society; in the context of globalisation and its corrosive effects on the nation-state; of technological change; and of the effects of the globalised and then re-localised media. Our notions of who we are and who we should be have been deeply formed by the nation-state, and by its homogenising attempts to produce a uniform 'national subject'; that fact is only now beginning to become apparent when the nation-state is under the severest stress. Curricula need to respond sensitively and responsibly to these facts.

Above all, there are forces at work at the moment which threaten if not the destruction of the means of cultural and intellectual and moral regeneration, then certainly the impoverishment of these resources of our cultural futures. These forces are the by-product of what later in the book I call 'Fast Capitalism' – shallow notions of accountability, effectiveness, efficiencies; the unchecked effects of the market; and the spread of its baleful practices into cultural and intellectual life. The futures which are proposed at the moment, either explicitly, implicitly, or by default, are not the only futures which can be imagined, even within (Fast) Capitalism. It is here where the English curriculum can, in its contents and resources, project a vision of another future, a 'working future'. English is the curriculum of communication and of representation, among others, and in its treatment of the practices of communication, as of the practices of representation, the texts, the visions we make, and how we make them, it holds, implicitly, the most decisive power for the making of working futures.

The English teacher as intellectual, and the making of the public domain

One of my own aims is to move beyond critique as an aim in itself, to the proposal of alternatives as a new and necessary aim; in which critical ability is an essential component. This comes from a recognition of my own past reluctance to do more than offer critique. Indeed, two kinds of academic work that I have been associated with – Critical Linguistics, and Critical Discourse Analysis – are instances of precisely that. It seems to me inescapable now that I have a responsibility, as an academic, to go beyond that, and to participate actively in the shaping of the world, in the area of my competence. That has always been the role of the intellectual in Europe, where that includes all those who work with the intellect: journalists, publishers, teachers, politicians, doctors, academics, artists, writers, etc. It is not a term which feels comfortable in the Anglo-Saxon context; nevertheless, I would like to propose using it. For one thing, it unites the concerns of a large group, and it makes me able to think of my work as an academic as being connected with the work of teachers in their classrooms: working in our distinctive domains, and yet united in a broader project.

There is a further reason for moving beyond critique. Critique is essential in periods of social stability as a means of producing change; by bringing that which is settled into crisis, it is a means for producing a cultural dynamic. In periods of intense change the problem is that the cultural dynamic is too great, so that critique is not the issue; the focus of intervention has to shift to the design of possible alternatives.

The move has a liberating effect; it allows us to focus on shared, broader social and cultural aims – in some ways entirely old-fashioned and traditional – and questions: what is education for? who is education for? what is the English curriculum *for*?

English, alone among the subjects which form the core of the National Curriculum, is peculiar in that it has no discipline 'standing behind' it. Science has Science; Mathematics has Mathematics. English has what? This places a huge burden on the curriculum, and explains in part at least, the ferocity which has characterised its recent history – compared to that of those other subjects. It also places an enormous burden on English teachers, who become the sole bearers of that edifice of largely unarticulated but all the more strongly *felt* cultural assumptions about English, about what it should be, and do.

From a pedagogic point of view it is the English teacher's role, like that of any teacher, to make accessible knowledges, materials and resources which a child can use in their own making of themselves as a human social subject. The question, however, is precisely this: what kind of social subject do we imagine, and what therefore should these knowledges, materials, resources be? In other words: what is English? and what does the English curriculum have as its goal for the young people who experience it? I'll attempt an answer to the first question first, in hugely abbreviated form.

English *is* a number of curricula, around which the English teacher has to construct some plausible principles of coherence. It is, first, a curriculum of communication, at the moment largely via its teaching around English language. As I will point out later, this curriculum is coming into crisis, with the move in public communication from language to the visual and from 'mind' to the body. It is, second, a curriculum of notions of sociality and of culture: what England is, what it is to be English. This is carried through a plethora of means: how the language English is presented and talked about, especially in multilingual classrooms; what texts appear and how *they* are dealt with; what theories of text and language underlie pedagogies; and so on.

English is also a curriculum of values, of taste, and of aesthetics. Here the study of canonical texts is crucial, in particular their valuation in relation to texts of popular culture – media texts, the 'fun' materials children use in their lives – and in relation to the texts of cultural groups of all kinds. This raises the fundamental issue of the rethinking of leisure and of work, and a re-evaluation of what it is that provides pleasure for humans. And so, importantly, English is the subject in which ethics, questions of social, public morality are constantly at issue: not in terms of the imposition of 'right' ways of thinking, but in terms of giving children the means of dealing with ethical, moral issues on the one hand and by absorbing, and perhaps this is most important, the ethos developed in the classroom.

What this means is that there is no aspect of practice in the English classroom which is not laden with social significance. If, in the science laboratory, an experiment does not come off, or misfires, the teacher will have a problem establishing a scientific principle. If, in the English classroom, a text is 'misread', it has lasting social consequences. In the English classroom there are no second chances.

1 Future gazing

Some things personal

I left England in 1978, after working here for some eleven years, to take up a job in Australia. When I returned in mid-1991 quite a few things had changed. One of my first, quite shocking impressions were some newspaper clippings passed on to me by a friend, around the just completed LINC (Language in the National Curriculum) materials. One of these contained a diatribe against a group of 'ideologically motivated' people; they were characterised as being anti-racist, anti-sexist and multicultural, bent on subverting the education system. Coming fresh from Australia I blinked, literally, to see 'anti-racist', 'anti-sexist' and 'multicultural' used as terms of abuse. What hole had I fallen through?

Some months later a group of visiting Russians delivered themselves of a confident judgement on the state in contemporary Britain as being like that of the Stalinist Soviet Union. Stalin, it may be remembered, intervened in a bitter debate that had broken out among Soviet linguists in the 1930s on the question of dialect. He pronounced that in a classless society there could be no (social) dialects; and so settled a seemingly difficult argument immediately and decisively. The winners returned to their jobs; the losers were wandered off to the East, most to perish there. Of course, I realised, in the Britain of the 1990s there was no racism; so only trouble-makers could be interested, mischievously, in stirring up trouble by pretending that there was. It was a sharp introduction to some of the educational facts of life (to say 'educational debate' for exchanges at that time seems too severe a shift for that term).

But what contribution could *I* make here, an outsider in so many ways? After all, this was the first time I had found myself 'in' Education: I had just left a job in Media, Cultural, and Communication Studies, in Sydney. Yes, during a previous period in England I had worked while I was teaching at the University of East Anglia in the 1970s with colleagues at Keswick College of Education; and on returning to Australia, in 1978, to Adelaide, I went to a former College of Education which was turning itself into a multi-purpose institution. While I was involved in that, I taught some courses in the Education faculty. Then, in Sydney, from 1983 to 1991, I had been closely involved in the literacy research that has since become known and influential as the 'Genre-school'. And yes, I had written a book on how children learn to write. But all of that was done from the outside, on the margin of Education, in a very real sense.

I myself saw my interest in Education as entirely of a piece with my interest in Cultural Studies, though with quite far-reaching extensions. As one of the significant sites of cultural reproduction, Education must be of interest to anyone concerned with culture and with society. For me, that link was defined around issues of subjectivity and identity, who we are, how we make ourselves. But I was an outsider too, in returning to England from Australia after a thirteen-year absence, having missed – except for annual visits – the entire Thatcher period. How could I attempt to engage in a struggle that had gone on for that length of time, and with such astonishing ferocity from one side in this encounter? What claim could I have? What right, what experience? Clearly, the answer on one level was: none.

And yet. Sometimes the outsider – who has no choice but to see things differently – may have a perspective which can be helpful. I began to feel quickly, with the confidence that only ignorance can bestow, that the debate was conducted in inappropriate terms, on both sides. On the one side there was the argument, familiar to me from Australia, of the failure of the Education system to deliver economic success to the nation, and demands, therefore, for Education to be reformed and re-aligned to serve the needs of business, of commerce, and of industry. Even the details of the argument were familiar: literacy levels were declining, costing the economy billions of dollars/pounds, in lost income, etc.

That much was dispiritingly the same. What was different was the ferocity of the ideological attack on Education, on teachers, on teacher trainers and on – a term I hadn't encountered before – the 'Education establishment'. Nor was I familiar with the quite explicit contents of that bit of the attack: a case, expressed in different ways – whether about teaching methods, literary texts to be taught, about reading or grammar – for a resolute about-turn, a decision to march back to the mythic certainties of a fabled golden age, some time back there in the reign of Queen Victoria.

This purely ideological project I hadn't encountered in Australia: nor could I have. Driven, as it was (dare I use the past tense?) by uncontrollable nostalgias of various kinds, it couldn't, of course, be a project in a country where the past is most decidedly not a place to look back on with nostalgia, let alone attempt to return to: the past, in Australia, of a brutally harsh origin, brutally enforced by the new, white population on itself, and even more brutally on the Aboriginal population. There the project is that of the building of a new society, founded on the commonality of a shared *place*, founded too on the real and remarkable achievements by men and women, over two centuries; of inventiveness and sheer hard work; of a broadly supportive, egalitarian ethos, the willingness to let anyone have a fair go (an account which sets aside, over this period, the deeply dark history of white treatment of the Aboriginal population until very recent times).

But above all, and most decisively, the various strands of the broad ideological, social, educational project of the political right in England seemed to me to be beside the point if the real question is that of the political, social and economic futures and needs of Britain in the early parts of the twenty-first century. The rhetoric around assumed Victorian certainties could only serve to accelerate the starkly apparent signs of social division, disintegration, and of economic decline.

Some things prospective

A curriculum is a design for the future. That is its most crucial characteristic, among many others. A curriculum provides, even if entirely implicitly, the knowledge, the principles, and the modes of thinking, the possibilities of action which form the stuff with which, around which, and out of which young people can, if they wish, make themselves as social subjects. A curriculum projects a vision of the future, and it is that aspect which forms the basis for the examination of present curricula, and of any changes and reforms which are proposed. This seems to me to provide a relatively secure perspective from which to conduct an investigation, an analysis, and an argument for new directions. From this perspective the rigidities and the narrowness, the dispositions of an uncritical stance towards knowledge, the acceptance of authority which are implied in some of the worst rhetorical flourishes of ideologues on the right, seemed to me so far out of line with the kind of personality needed for productive social futures for this society, that only despair or incredulity, outrage or bitter laughter seem to offer a possible response.

But while this was not a programme for anything other than at best 'the management of civilised decline' (to use the words of a senior figure in the Conservative Party during a television interview), I found no real focus on social and economic futures in the arguments on the other side. Here there were – and I sense no longer *are* in the same way – implicit allegiances to a personality corresponding to the enlightened notions of the 1960s and early 1970s. If I attempted to draw out the assumptions of that project they would be two: a neo-romantic expressive individualism on the one hand, and a deeply unrecognised and, paradoxically, unacknowledged notion of a homogenous, and ethnically monocultural society.

This may seem a gross misreading on my part, given the real commitment of those who have worked so strongly in support and encouragement of multilingualism in schools. Yet the sign of a monocultural curriculum is its implicit adherence to the idea of a universal human subject, so that one outward sign of monoculturalism is an implicit curriculum. The one supports the other. However implicitly, both depend on and are underpinned by notions of the nation-state, and by its ideas of 'national character', the assumption of shared national characteristics, whether of 'Australianness', of 'Englishness', of 'Welshness'. If I assume that all my students are, in some way and at some essential level, the same, I can sustain an inexplicit curriculum. If values and knowledges are shared by all, then of course I do not need to make them explicit.

In that sense the introduction of *the idea* of a national curriculum was a fundamental challenge. While on the surface it seemed most of all to be a challenge to the teacher's authority and professionalism, in a real sense it was a more fundamental challenge to the implicitly held notions of the homogeneous, monocultural nation (where the real issues of class had not been allowed to emerge into examinations and the curricula leading to them) and its homogeneous subjectivities which could be coaxed into full development by the application of the right personal and cultural nourishment. Of course, this exposes a deep paradox on the government's side. Its idea was that the National Curriculum would re-instate, re-affirm a set of homogeneous, nationally shared knowledges and values. But that attempt arose precisely out of a realisation that no such homogeneous set of values any longer existed. The fact that they never had was, from that point of view, beside the point. It is ironic at the very least that it was a government dedicated to the revival of national identity and values that recognised the realities of fragmentation and difference.

The introduction of the National Curriculum has moved the agenda decisively from the *now* to the *future*. This has not been recognised or spoken about overtly. The debate has proceeded very much in terms of *present* economic, commercial needs; although the ideological aspects of the debate have addressed the issue in terms of a return to the values of that more certain past – whether of the 1950s, the 1920s and 1930s, or of the nineteenth century. In one sense even this is still a future project: to remake the young in the image of a mythic past. Thus equipped, Britain would face the challenges of the twenty-first century.

The significance of the debates around the National Curriculum lies, in the end, around the attempt to produce a social subject, a future citizen, with the attributes implied in the forms and contents of the curriculum. The fact that there has been no unanimity about that set of values is not in the least surprising. The curriculum has had to be constructed to accommodate the multifarious, often competing demands of a variety of factions: business wanting effective communicators; finance needing technologically competent users of electronic communications; the far right seeking a population which – apart from a small élite – would be socially tractable; high-level administrators seeking a perpetuation of an administrative and bureaucratic élite; and so on.

But these are all couched in terms of present understandings of the present. What is needed, quite decisively now, is an attempt to speculate about the near future, the future of the next two decades or three, the period for which the generation now in schools is being educated; and the period which will decisively map out the social, economic and political future of Britain for the next hundred years. There is in my mind the haunting possibility of the histories of (the former empires of) Spain and Portugal, a history of three hundred years of relentless decline, from which both are only now beginning to emerge. It has become imperative, therefore, to spell out alternative conceptions of that future.

This is an intensely political issue entirely beyond party-politics; as with that other great topic, Europe, I imagine that this issue of social futures produces alignments which cross party-political divides. It is an issue on which the most serious and wide-ranging debate is to be had. The curriculum must attempt to match the demands of that tomorrow in what it provides today. Of course, the shape of that tomorrow can only be a best guess, made in the light of that debate. Nevertheless, some principles are becoming clearer. And so there cannot be, at the moment, a stipulation about precise contents of a curriculum. That will, on the one hand, have to wait for the outcome of that broadly inclusive and later more detailed debate. And it will, on the other hand, have to be subject to regular re-assessment. Some principles are clear to me. It is to some elaboration of these that this small volume is given over.

Principles for writing the future

Two sets of principles form the substance of debate in my view. One has to do with the political, cultural, economic characteristics of our imagined social futures and of essential characteristics of individuals living in that future. If in outlining principles for a curriculum we are sketching the framework of a Utopia, we need to say what we think its basic features are or should be. Honesty requires no less. The second set of principles has to do with our skills in imagining the shape of developments, socially, economically, technologically, culturally, and with our speculation from these as to the likely means of getting from the here and now to that future form of society, and of its citizens. On the one hand the new curriculum will be an attempt to provide the future citizens of that society with the skills, dispositions, aptitudes and characteristics to lead productive lives; and on the other hand, the curriculum is our attempt to *participate*, actively, in the shaping of that future.

This is a new and unusual role, for teachers as for academics; the Anglo-Saxon mode has been one of pragmatic involvement in pursuing a set of aims, and, where needed, of offering critique. My suggestion is for our active engagement in the design and making of that future.

Let me outline, sketchily, the first of my set of principles. Paramount for me is the principle that our children and their children should live in a world which offers them the possibilities of productive, fulfilling lives, as productive, fulfilling and rich as my life has been for me. I realise that there is no absolute measure of these things; they have varied historically, and will continue to do so. Yet humans can always say whether their lives have dignity, fulfilment, and happiness. I realise too that the requirements of ecologically sustainable futures may well mean some reduction in material circumstances, which may be compensated for by other, non-materialistic aspects of human social lives. This places ethical and moral demands on the curriculum; in particular an envisioning of a return to forms of production in which individuals have some significant responsibility: whether in relation to the production of material objects; services to others; or of cultural and intellectual goods.

The second of my set of principles touches on imagining the world of tomorrow. I cannot imagine that the trends towards pluriculturalism will be reversed; I believe that they will intensify. The simple facts of globalisation, and of the technologies of transport, make it inevitable. The gradual disintegration of nation-states which we are witnessing at the moment will continue, and, I think, accelerate: not only in Europe, but in many parts of the world. The politics of difference have produced a socially corrosive dynamic; as has the electronically achieved globalisation of the economy – both in finance and in manufacture; so has the transnationalisation of the now transcultural media, whether mass-broadcast, or individualised and narrowcast. All three are intensified and speeded up by the intranational pluriculturalism of ever more ethnically diverse societies. And so, included in my second set of principles is that that world will have to be one in which difference is seen as a resource for productive lives and for innovative encounters with problems. The English curriculum, perhaps alone among the subjects in the National Curriculum, can address this issue. It has the possibility of showing difference as productive, of showing the dynamics of change as normal and natural, and of developing dispositions in which humans can be and are active and responsible for their lives and for the well-being of their communities.

In my speculations I feel certain of some things: technological change will not slow down over the next two decades; the globalisation of economies will accelerate; societies will become more diverse; ethnic and social differences will not become a lesser factor, politically and culturally; media and culture will at one and the same time both be global and yet, given the replacement of the traditional mass-media by media products aimed at the niche, cultural production will simultaneously be more local in its articulation.

These factors have global effects, and yet will have quite specific, and markedly divergent, effects in particular localities. A post-imperial society and economy such as that of Britain is differently placed, for instance, to a newly emergent post-colonial society and economy such as Australia. But what is crucial, from this point of view, is that such considerations now have to form an absolutely central concern of curriculum planning and construction. Added to this is the question of how these factors of change will have their impacts in relation to the histories and the traditions of any one country. From such considerations arises a set of concerns for the curriculum which simply must be faced, in ways in which the English curriculum has never yet been discussed.

A nation such as England cannot contemplate with any degree of equanimity a slide into continuing economic decline, a future as the Bangladesh of Europe, even though current economic policies and attitudes suggest this as a real possibility: the social dislocations would, simply, be cataclysmic. But if this is a future that we do not wish to contemplate, then the only real other future is one in which Britain once again sees itself as a leader in culture; in commerce; in production. Britain's history over the last three centuries in Europe and in the world has been that of a leader in the domain of social, economic and political development; it led Europe into the age of Enlightenment, and of democratic government, and into the Industrial Revolution. That history is there to be recovered and to be built upon. To do so Britain will need to re-build an economy based on a culture of innovation, on a culture which draws on what is now the major economic resource of this country: its people, and the fabulous resources of the diversity of its population.

Working futures: English in the age of Fast Capitalism

These are issues which have not formed the usual concerns of English teachers – nor of academics in universities for that matter. I want to suggest that they are absolutely central: if a curriculum is a design for a future human subject, a future citizen and, through them, for a future society, then these are the starting points for every discussion of curriculum. That may be strange and new, but it is essential.

Although it has perhaps a disturbing tone to it, my message is old-fashioned, and traditional. The older values of English which I mentioned earlier did, of course, envisage a particular kind of human being as the outcome of education; that part is not new. What *appears* new is the fact that we are no longer envisioning human subjects for a stable society with a stable present, or for a knowable future, for a future which is in all essentials like the present (a factor which led us to forget the historical specificity of that human subject). Rather, we are producing human, social subjects in a rapidly changing period, for a future which is likely to undergo ever more radical change. Many of the values which I advocate are not new: they have formed a part of liberal humanistic education for decades, for much of the century. They are the values of intellectual curiosity, of flexibility, analytic sophistication, adaptability, that is, the ability to bring quite general categories to bear on specific issues, and to deal with these in varying circumstances. They are the values that have characterised English teaching for several decades now.

Where my message *is* new is in its attempts to think of curriculum overtly and directly in relation to likely social, economic, political changes, in relation to likely futures, and in its thinking of the English curriculum as a central means of *intervention*, as a crucial factor in participating in the construction of those futures. A major task in this is to sort the essential wheat from the ideological chaff. There is a deep difficulty in understanding what, in contemporary social and economic developments, is real rather than purely ideological. Of course, both the 'real' and the ideological have effects, and both interact, though differentially, with the traditions of a society; in and with those traditions of English teaching which we may wish to retain even if in a transformed manner.

Much of what has gone on in English teaching needs to be retained: the future cannot be made from nothing, even if we wanted to do so. What appears as *new making* is always the transformation of existing practices, materials and structures, in the light and the needs of new conditions. So here I will sketch some of the rudiments of the social and economic aspects of the new, in order to understand what transformations of the existing forms we may need to undertake.

First I consider aspects of the economic; after that I will, in turn, consider aspects of the cultural and the technological. I will name this *economic new* by the label given to it by some of its prophets: Fast Capitalism. Fast Capitalism is the capitalism of Milton Friedmann (and of his various local adaptations in the shape of Thatcher, Reagan, Hawke, Keating and others), speeded up by the application of electronic technologies. The latter enable money to be moved around the globe, literally, at the speed of light, in a global market which never sleeps.

Fast Capitalism has relied on the English language as the essential carrier of its viral infection, so that non-English-speaking capitalist economies have been either relatively immune or affected by a milder strain of the virus only: examples are Japanese capitalism, and so-called Rhineland capitalism. Unlike the latter two, Fast Capitalism is entirely shareholder and dividend driven, so that its aims and goals are short-term goals, from one annual shareholder meeting to the next, from one dividend distribution round to the one following. There is no wish for, or possibility of, longer-term strategies. Its responsibilities are not therefore to the development and building of viable bases of production, to investment whether through capital or in research, nor to the careful development of markets, nor to outdated notions such as 'communities'. So its responsibilities are not to the local context or even to the national, but to short-term considerations of profit. Fast Capitalism is highly mobile; capital and finance are seen in global terms, and this makes jobs mobile. They can be 'exported', as when production facilities are re-located to a lower wage environment; or imported, when this is useful, as with inward investment into the UK by Japanese electronics or motor manufacturers in order, in this instance, to gain access to European markets.

With mobility comes a 'downward' redistribution of accountability; hierarchies are obstacles to mobility. Mobility fragments the 'workplace' into unitary elements which are accountable as individualised 'cost-' and 'profit-centres', accountable individually for their productive efficiencies. The elimination of hierarchical management structures carried forward with the aim of achieving 'flat management structures' is both a goal and an effect of accountability at the level of individual cost-centre units. Middle management becomes redundant in this process: its supervisory function is taken over by a new machinery and by the process of inculcating the ideals and values of 'corporate culture'. The individual as an efficient cost-centre thus becomes a self-regulating production unit through the regulatory effects of the internalised values of corporate culture, proclaimed and reified in the 'The Mission Statement'. Each member of a corporation is his or her own middle manager; the accountant of their own cost-centre; and their own profit-centre.

The internalisation of corporate values as the individual's own ('assuming/taking ownership') eliminates the possibilities of a distinction of private and public domains; workers become corporate entities for twenty-four hours a day. The ideal becomes one where private lives and public practices are conducted in terms of the same corporate culture, with the same identity. One positive construction that can be put on this state of affairs is that this gives the individual freedom, 'ownership' of their work practices, of their workplace responsibilities, responsibility for their own actions. But this is both the responsibility to succeed, and the freedom to fail. The realities are that there are flatter structures of decision-making, that the possibilities of participation have increased, and may be real. But the overriding values of 'accountability' at the *individual* level mean that corporate profit and profitability set absolute limits to freedom.

It is difficult to know what the 'real' of this situation is. It is *not* merely ideological: the electronic workings of globalised finance-capital do mean that jobs can be and are exported with enormous rapidity to low-wage environments. In turn, this means that jobs are much more mobile than actual humans, people; and in one sense *their* only real mobility is to become more mobile in terms of efficiencies, measured in the terms of accountability of corporate culture and measured in terms of redeployability. For most employees this means a downward mobility, into casualised, part-time, semi-skilled work. And as East or South Asian economies move to becoming higher labour-cost economies, other lower-cost economies are found.

There are alternatives. The Gurus of Fast Capitalism do not look beyond the boundaries of the corporation – in as far as it is transnational there seems to them to be no relevance to the local environment: the local is a mere accident, or it can, seemingly, be treated as such. However, Japanese or Rhineland capitalism both show that this is not a necessary effect of capitalism as such, but that it is an effect of one kind of capitalism. The destruction of the social and natural environment of the localities of particular corporations may, even in the medium term, prove deleterious to the effective working of Fast Capitalist corporations. The willed short-sightedness of the Gurus of Fast Capitalism is, of course, no reason why others should not, and indeed must not, begin to think about the forms of larger social organisation within which corporations exist. The elevation of social irresponsibility into a corporate good – or even into a publicly proclaimed ethic – has a logic within Fast Capitalism. Corporations can live for a time, parasitically, off the social (and cultural and economic) infrastructures produced by the societies in which they choose to site their factories, warehouses, design studios, research centres, assemblage plants. There is every reason why the communities which are the – often unwilling – hosts of these corporations should develop their own ethic and from that, *their* demands for their social group.

It is entirely possible, and it is becoming essential, to begin to engage in the imaginative construction of new forms of sociality. That this can be done jointly *with* capitalism is demonstrated in many parts of the (too often non-Anglo) world. My argument here is not against corporate capitalism, but against a form of Fast Capitalism which does not concern itself with anything beyond the boundary of the corporation. It is in the end a straightforward question of whose priorities are to carry the day: those of humans living in particular localities, or of corporations with merely global perspectives, and with the ethics of the pirate.

The inherently positive values promulgated by the prophets of Fast Capitalism – ownership, responsibility, participation, valuation of individual contribution and difference – often work in an entirely proper and serious fashion within some corporations, and have brought satisfaction to the working lives of many. These values need to be projected beyond the boundaries of the corporation, to imagined ways of social organisation of communities, and there to be promulgated without the too often deleterious aspects of that same set of values, the dark underside of this form of corporation.

This is an argument about the English curriculum, and not one about economics. The question I am posing is simply this: in relation to economic (and social) futures such as these, what is the English curriculum doing? And what could or should it be doing? Does it, in the end, have any relevance at all, beyond the relatively superficial ones which are foregrounded in public debate now? For me, the answer is clear: only the English curriculum can engage with these absolutely fundamental issues: if jobs are movable with the speed of electricity on global fiscal markets, then certain requirements of a fundamental kind follow for the kind of person whom we are preparing for that world. Somehow they will have to be prepared not just to cope, but to control their circumstances.

I will make some suggestions, both of a very general kind, and give some quite specific instances in other parts of this small book. Here I will say just this: certain proposals advanced around the English curriculum from ideological positions of the far right imply orientations to authority which simply seem implausible to me as means for coping with that future. In the Anglo-Saxon world we are presently dealing with the problems of social, economic and technological change with theories – and social nostrums – deeply embedded in a common-sense which derives from the very beginning of the Industrial Revolution, two hundred years ago. We cannot hope to solve ethical issues of work, human fulfilment, employment, leisure, with the theories which ushered in the transition from agrarian feudalism to industrialism. But to produce the necessary new theories and the cultural values, we need human, social subjects able to live without anxiety in times of change, for whom sharp critique is an inevitable aspect of an innovative, productive stance. That productive stance entails moving from critique as one of the traditional aims of a humanistic education to the design of alternatives – socially, culturally, politically, as well as economically and technologically. Alone among school subjects, English has the possibility of addressing the issue of what kind of human dispositions are crucial for the achievements of such aims.

Cultural futures

Most human societies have experienced periods of pronounced multi- or polyculturalism in their histories; some of these have been more profound than that in our own period. This is as true of Africa as it is of Asia, of Europe as of America. The final centuries of the Roman Empire saw the profoundest ethnic changes in Europe and around the Mediterranean. What is different now is the coincidence of vast population shifts with the globalisation of transport, economies, and communication and information and cultural systems. Among the latter I am thinking, of course, of the media in particular.

The existence of global means of cultural dissemination adds an entirely new element to multiculturalism (and to multilingualism). It ensures that pluriculturalism is here to stay, that it will intensify, and that it is linked into all aspects of public life: economic, political, social; and all aspects of the private. This pluriculturalism therefore exists within a particular social or national entity and outside or beyond it. Both have profound effects on the formation of human subjectivity and identity, and through this on our social, cultural and economic futures. On the one hand 'internal' pluriculturalism presents enormous challenges to the coherence and integrity of nation-states; on the other hand it offers the solutions to the very problems which these societies are facing. One of the central issues is how any one society or nation positions itself, what 'stance' it takes *vis-a-vis* the issue of pluriculturalism. In this it is of fundamental importance to understand the histories through which a society has come to 'be' multicultural. I have some knowledge of three multicultural societies – Australia, England, Germany – in different ways and to different degrees, and I will use this here as a relatively intuitive means of outlining my ideas on this question.

At first sight, anyone walking through the streets of Sydney, or London, or Frankfurt, will note that they all 'are' or 'look' multicultural: on a closer look we will notice that the composition of the population in the street differs somewhat from place to place. That is a first indicator of different histories. In London, faces from the Caribbean and from the Indian subcontinent are most noticeable; in Frankfurt there is a greater presence of people from the Mediterranean and the Middle East perhaps; and in Sydney, now, South East Asian faces are strongly present: along with – in all three places – many other groups.

The social position, and hence the potential cultural effectiveness, of a group depends on their history in that society. There is, as an example, an immediately noticeable difference between the relative openness, or not, towards the idea of a multicultural society in Sydney, and in London or Frankfurt. That appears in many different ways: as I have mentioned already, in forms of the curriculum for instance. Another indicator is a concern with 'identity': 'who we are'. In Australia that is now a real question: 'What is Australia?' 'What is it to be an Australian?' No dinner party passes without a debate about this in some form or other; no issue of any national newspaper doesn't have some reference to it. It is a question which is absent in England, except possibly in relation to the issue of the integrity of the UK, *vis-a-vis* the (potential) desire for autonomy on the part of Wales or Scotland, which would involve a re-thinking of 'Englishness'.

Similarly in Frankfurt. The presence of five to six million former 'guest workers' does not lead to a questioning of identity, of what it is to be 'German'; that question arises there in relation to the issue of 'Europe', and the place and meaning of 'Germanness' in that context.

The potential effects and effectiveness of 'other' cultures in a society are affected and regulated by that issue: if identity is not on the agenda, then 'otherness' is just 'otherness'. The possibilities of a mutual redefinition, of real interaction, and a reworking of a new 'mainstream' are circumscribed, or non-existent for the time being. However, that is not the whole story. 'Other' cultures have been accepted relatively easily, readily, and positively into the Australian mainstream; yet their cultural contribution (beyond the usual outward signs: restaurants, types of food in shops, etc.) has been relatively slight. In Britain, where acceptance has been, to my eyes, much more provisional, much more tentative, the cultural impact of the Black, Caribbean community in particular is enormous: it sets the agenda, largely, of that part of the culture which is most prominent, most alive, most effective: in music, in clothing, in language. By contrast, the populations from the Indian subcontinent have not, until relatively recently, had a similar impact, though that seems now to be changing. What has caused that difference? Why is it, to put that question more starkly, that Turkish culture is not having any real cultural effects in Germany? In my view one has to look to the different histories which have brought a particular cultural group into a social place, and attempt to understand, from there, what contribution the group is making, what contribution it could or should be making.

Unless we understand that, we cannot hope to bring the resource of cultural diversity into productive use. So the question is: what is the history, in detail, of multiculturalism here, in this place, and what therefore are the possibilities, the challenges, and the barriers? A far too general and crude account of this in the case of England would look to the very different conditions of immigration, first of the people from the Caribbean, who saw themselves – during a colonial period – as full members of the Empire (and then of the Commonwealth), most of them usually speaking English as their first language, and understanding Englishness even if in local adaptations and as a result of deep struggles; integrated into the workforce in England in a particular way, and at a time when this was *relatively* unproblematic. Their perception of their stake in that new place was, I imagine, different to that of the populations from the Indian subcontinent, also with their – quite different – colonial experience of Britain; a deeply different experience, for instance, speaking not English but one of the languages of the subcontinent as their first language and having, in their original place, cultural histories extending further back by far than those of the colonisers.

In my view multiculturalism is, quite simply, a fact for English society, and if anything it will intensify. At the very least, prudent social and cultural planning demands that all members of all cultural groups be given a real stake in this society, an interest in its common prospering and health. At best, the issue of equity will begin to be seen in quite different ways, as I suggested earlier, in ways in which the productive potential of cultural difference comes to the fore, where each cultural group is seen as having resources of equal value to all other groups, absolutely central to the success of society as a whole. This is where the English curriculum has its crucial role to play, and where I believe English, alone among the subjects in the National Curriculum, can have and must offer its fundamental contribution. It is here where curriculum needs to be thought about in terms of the kinds of resources which must be made available to children, and to young men and women – cultural and linguistic resources; and needs to be discussed in terms of how they will need to be presented, in order to enable that self-making of young humans: as confident with change, not anxious in the face of deep difference, but seeing these, rather, as normal, positive, and as essential resources for the making of fulfilling lives, in a society and culture built on innovation.

Technologies

There is a tendency, less strong now perhaps than ten years or so ago, to see technology as an independently active agent in human social affairs. Of course it is not: unless the social conditions are right – whatever complexities hide behind that simplification – a technology will not be adopted, will not succeed. Yet technologies are powerful, in their social deployment and in their culturally transformative effects. The technology of literacy – of lettered representation – is a case in point. It provided, compared with 'orality', a fundamentally different cultural logic to the societies which employed it, which became literate – a shift from the logic of sequence in time of speech, to the logic of hierarchy in (actual or abstract) space of writing. Many, perhaps most, of what are regarded as criterial characteristics of contemporary technologically developed societies, can be traced to the potentials of this technology and of its logics.

Electronic technologies are having effects on the potentials of communication which are as yet incalculable, but seem already at least as far-reaching in their potential effects as the shift from orality to literacy, or the newer shift from literacy to 'visuality'. Their deep effects are noticeable in several domains: in unmaking and remaking social relations; in their potential effects on the basis of the rule-system of language; in their unmaking and remaking of ideas of writing and reading; of authorship and readership; and perhaps, in the end, though not as yet fully recognised, on the place of language in the landscape of communication, in the semiotic landscape overall.

All of these have effects in the area in which English operates. Let me expand on them briefly here, in turn. Take the question of social relations. The relative formality of writing derives in part from 'distance' – of the geographical and temporal distance of writer and addressee, but also, most usually, of social distance: when I write, I usually relate with an absent reader in a relation in which the formality of some institutional or role relationship is foregrounded. Electronic mail undoes this distance: it brings about the temporal (even if not geographical) proximity of speech, and with that it brings even the social proximity of speech into what is still a *written* interaction – except that this writing now begins to unravel in terms of its most writing-like characteristics, and begins to look much more speech-like in its grammatical and syntactic form.

At the same time, this same technology dissolves the social distinction of writer and reader. Traditionally, the writer produced a text to be read by many; hence the position of the writer was inherently more powerful than that of the reader. Now, writing is, on the one hand, often for *one* immediate recipient, which introduces a newer kind of equality; on the other hand, I as the reader can, even with contemporarily available technologies, immediately make my reading visible in my re-writing of the initial/initiating text. This also diminishes (or nearly negates) the power of the writer: it is now – or can be – a mutual activity, in which reading has (very nearly) become real writing.

The categories of writing, writer, author, as of reading, reader, have for so long served as crucial if implicit underpinnings of the English curriculum, that their dissolution will have far-reaching effects. The status of the author, of authority, as of authorship, are suddenly democratised, made ordinary.

This same set of effects is simultaneously changing the status of text: joint-authoring has, for some time, been a theoretical notion, for instance as the idea of texts as 'multi-voiced'. It has been a practice, a theoretical as well as a pedagogical notion in English classrooms. Indeed, it has been a practice, though more laboriously, in many places of text-making: the joint production of a pamphlet or a report, or a book. Now it is a reality in that truly co-operative, communal writing is now easily possible, a 'natural' effect of the technology, and from this time on the notion of 'ownership', of authenticity, and so on are difficult to maintain. The privileged, mythic, sacred status of the text and its author is unmade more effectively by this technology than by the theoretical writings of clever semioticians.

English has not been the sole property of the English for a considerable time now. It is estimated that between 1 and 1.5 billion people may be using English either as a first language or as a preferred language. Given that the population of Great Britain is around 55 million, it is clear that British English is now a minority form – though still with great cultural cachet in many places around the globe. However, in trade, in the global economy generally, British English is not the form used. East Asian and American, perhaps even African and Central European forms of English predominate. But can this, will this have an effect on English in England? Will it not remain simply as a fact about 'global English'? In my view it will not. Apart from the usual effects of power – the fact that the forms of the powerful carry the day, as has been said before in slightly different form – it is again the appearance of technology that has its effects here. We have already become totally used to the situation where young people in England are addressed by commercial radio, for instance, in a dialect decidedly west of the mid-Atlantic ridge; no one even notices that in many genres of popular music an American accent is *de rigueur*, is the unnoticed norm.

But these are merely the beginnings of the intervention of technology. The big prize to be won in this field is direct voice–computer interaction. For that to happen certain technological advances in computing power have yet to be made. These will not be made in the UK, nor probably even in the US. They will be made somewhere in East Asia. However, while one major problem is that of hardware (if that is still or will then still be an appropriate term), the truly monumental problem is a problem in linguistics: namely that of producing grammars which are subtle enough to be capable of parsing the 'natural' language, the language in use, and of phonological descriptions which will work as the analytic base of voice-recognition.

Let me pause on these two for a moment. The problems of machine-parsing of language are so vast that for the foreseeable future it is likely that only tightly controlled forms of language-use will be amenable to this processing. The grammars which will underlie this process of analysis will therefore be limited in two ways. One will be the inherent characteristics of the underlying theory of language, and of whatever limitations these will impart as 'natural' and in unrecognised form. The other will be the kind of language chosen. Both the former and the latter are unlikely to be helpful for the maintenance of English English; the former will most likely be based on a limiting amalgam of psychological/structuralist assumptions, about what language is, with some bits of pragmatics thrown in: derived, I venture to say, from theories produced in the US and in Japan. The latter will be a form of mid-Pacific English selected by those whose commercial and cultural focus is in the region of the

Pacific Rim. The 'hardware' will not be British; the grammar will be limiting; and the English will be based on non-English English models.

However, once introduced, this technological advance will immediately impose itself globally: just as the fax became essential within next to no time, this advance, with all its limitations, will be one that no corporation, no institution, no business will be able to do without. But it has the limitations that I mentioned: and as they cannot easily be overcome, users will have to adjust themselves, their voices, their syntax, to the technology. One of the scenarios of science-fiction, of machines speaking to each other in 'machine-language' will have become reality, except that humans will – as always – have to adapt themselves to the machines they have created. But these machines will be using a form of global English. Speakers of English in England (as elsewhere) will have to learn to use this form, until it comes as second nature. By then English in England will have become colonised by one of its offspring.

What is the time-scale for this scenario? I imagine that this technology will be commonplace in fifteen to twenty years time – perhaps sooner in some versions. What will be the effect on the English curriculum? The effect will be that the medium of communication which has given the subject its name will no longer be – in some central ways – English English. It is a consideration that needs to be factored into the new curriculum, in far-reaching ways.

This technology will also have far-reaching effects on what I have called the landscape of communication, the semiotic landscape. It is now commonplace that images are coming to be more and more dominant in many spheres of public communication. Look at the front page of *The Sun* and consider the amount of space given over to the (usually single) image; or to language in the form of screamer headlines; compared to language in its normal form. Most of us, and that includes myself, have forgotten, other than by a constant, deliberate act of recollection – that *The Sun* and the other tabloids did not always look as they now look. Their look is a very recent innovation: twenty years ago the front page of *The Sun* was covered in printed language.

The shift from language to image is not determined by technology, though technology has lent a powerful helping hand. The shift from language to the visual has profound social and political causes, of which multiculturalism/multilingualism is a central one, I assume.

Others have to do with changed notions of sociality, of citizenship, of work, of values, and so on. The changes to the front page of *The Sun* over the last twenty years or so can be read, in one sense, as an accurate record of the deep changes in (the British state's conception of) English society. It is not a wholly pleasant tale; though, again, in part, it is a tale also of real and positive changes.

However, this shift of the place of media in the semiotic landscape, from language to the visual, has received a powerful impetus from electronic technologies. While they have been quite readily adapted to word-processing, their uses extend far beyond that – as is well known – to the processing of information in any form, especially with rapid gain in computing power. In many ways these technologies are better adapted to the visual than to the verbal mode, and so in a very real sense they promise an era in which the visual may again become dominant over the verbal. We have been taught to forget that spoken language is not natural: it is an adaptation of organs devised for quite different purposes – preventing us from choking when we eat, allowing us to breathe, moving food through the mouth – to the purpose of communication through conversation. Its advantages are clear, in allowing your hands to move, for instance, while you're talking. But other modes are in use, even among humans: in sign languages, such as British Sign Language, gesture, based on the physical mobility of parts of the body, has been developed into a *fully* articulate system of communication. If electronic modes of communication do become dominant, the advantages of languages may quickly become specialised: I will communicate from my home with people around the globe visually/electronically, and with the people in my house, on certain occasions, verbally.

As computing power increases, the possibilities of multimodal communication accelerate. Whereas at the moment the visual and the verbal already co-exist on computer screens as much as on magazine pages, in the quite near future, sound – in the form of music or of 'soundtrack' – will be added. Texts have always been multimodal: a written text, for instance, is *laid out* in a particular way; it is produced using a particular *typeface, size, spacing*; it is produced on a certain *(quality of) paper*. All of these are independently meaningful systems of meaning (making). On the whole we have been taught to overlook this kind of multimodality, except in rare cases: 'How can you produce an essay on this scrappy bit of paper!' or 'This really looks good: full marks for presentation!' The new multimodality cannot be overlooked, even though we still look at texts through eyes trained in an older mode: which makes us still talk and think about images as 'illustrations', even when they fill five-sixths of a page and constitute the major mode of communication.

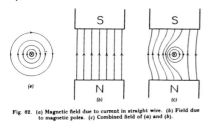

76   MAGNETISM AND ELECTRICITY

the magnetic poles. Fig. 62(c) shows the combined field of (a) and (b) when the wire is placed between the poles.

Note that, in Fig. 62(a) and (b), the lines of force on the left of the wire are in the same direction as those of the external field, while those on the right of the wire are in the opposite direction. Consequently in the combined field of Fig. 62(c) the field to the left of the wire is strong—there are a large number of lines, while the field to the right is weak.

If we assume, with Faraday, that the lines of force are in tension and trying to shorten (see p. 18), we should expect the wire to be urged to the right. This is precisely what we find by experiment.

Fig. 62. (a) Magnetic field due to current in straight wire. (b) Field due to magnetic poles. (c) Combined field of (a) and (b).

The principle of the electric motor.

The simple electric motor consists of a coil pivoted between the poles of a permanent magnet (see Fig. 63). When a current is passed through the coil in the direction indicated in the figure we can show, by applying Fleming's left-hand rule, that the left-hand side of the coil will tend to move down and the right-hand side of the coil to move up. (Remember that the direction of the field due to the permanent magnet is from the N. to the S. pole.) Thus the coil will rotate in a counter-clockwise direction to a vertical position.

Figure 1: *Image as illustration*

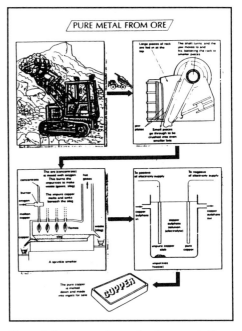

Figure 2: *Image as major mode of communication*

The two images here show the change. Figure 1 shows a page from a school text-book in which language is the central *medium of communication*, and the image functions as an illustration. By contrast, Figure 2 shows a page from a contemporary science text-book in which the visual has become the major mode of communication; language has now become a *medium of commentary*.

The new English curriculum will need to recognise these new forms of texts, with all their vast consequences, in their effects on the humans who make and use them. The currently dominant mode in relation to these changes is one of pessimism. Trained as we are, formed as subjects as we are in a culture in which the written was central, the move to the visual fills us with nostalgia and foreboding. That, however, is *our* problem: it is not the problem of the new generation unless we make it so, unless we make it our business to make them live their futures in the image of our pasts.

There are two cases to be made on the positive side, here. One has to do straightforwardly with the need to know what it is that the visual (or the multimodal) can do, that the verbal cannot; or vice-versa. This allows us a view, relatively freed from nostalgias, of what might be gained and what might be lost in this shift.

The other case concerns a reflection on the relation between forms of representation and communication, and the broad social and economic environment. One of the commonplaces about the present is the constant assertion of an 'information-explosion'. If it is indeed the case that information – in counterdistinction to *knowledge* – is being produced at a rate which is becoming or has already become unmanageable, then it may be the case that the verbal medium – whether spoken or written – will no longer suffice as a medium for the management of that information. It may be the case that the visual might. Our modes of apperception of information in the visual mode vary totally from those in the verbal. Imagine, as a simple example, the amount of information you process from the visual environment when you leave an underground station and step into the road; or when your arrive, latish, at a party, walk into a crowded room, and 'assess the situation'. How long would it take you to gain this information verbally, or to recount it, either in speech or in writing? The visual medium may be much better adapted to the near instantaneous apperception of vast amounts of information – much more efficient than language in the spoken or written form can be.

As our economic and technological environment changes it may be quite simply that we will need the visual as a basic, central medium of information management. The visual and the multimodal may represent the essential means of information management in the coming period. The English curriculum will need a stance on that.

That does not lead to an abandonment of concerns with language – it offers forms of rationality which we may wish or need to continue to foster, value, and develop – for those purposes for which it is best.

In my own hypothesis around these questions, forms of representation and forms of communication are totally at one with forms of subjectivity, identity, personality. The literate person, who gets fulfilment from the written text, whose modes of analysis, sustained over a long period, detailed, reflective, recursive, are formed in that medium, is a different person to the visual person, with a totally different stance in the world, different practices, different modes. If the curriculum is, as I suggest it is, a design for a future person, then these changes are of the highest significance.

The curriculum as design: Utopias and dystopias

At a time which seems to be actively inviting calamitous wreckage, I am interested in the construction of an Utopian vision. That vision, the construction of which will be the task of very many people over a considerable time, will be and can be put against present irrationalities, and act as a challenge and rebuttal, without being drawn onto the ground of someone else's designs.

Let me first of all state my principles again simply. These are first, that the curriculum should envisage, project, and aim to produce an individual who is at ease with difference and change, whose fundamental being values innovation and is therefore able to question, to challenge, and above all to *propose alternatives, constructively.* Implied in this is my second principle, that the curriculum should project and aim to take a central role in producing a society which values humans, accords them real dignity, and aims to provide for all its members the possibility of a quality of life which is at the least no worse than that enjoyed by my generation. As I said earlier, in this I do not necessarily envisage the same level of material benefits, but social and cultural values and practices which ensure a richly rewarding, and productive, life.

How is this to be translated into an English curriculum? Several questions arise. First, what is English now? And then, what will an English curriculum have to provide for children to give them the skills requisite for their productive tomorrows, implied in my principles? What kind of person do we imagine implicitly and explicitly as the ideal of this curriculum?

What is English, the school subject, now? What will it continue to be, given the overall structure of the whole National Curriculum? Here are some major aspects:

1. English is a carrier of definitions of culture.
2. English is a carrier of definitions of its society.
3. English, the language, is at the moment still the major medium of communication in this society, and the English curriculum must be fully cognisant of that.
4. The subject English is the only site in the curriculum where all the modes and media of public communication can be debated, analysed, and taught – there is nowhere else.
5. English is the site of the development of the individual in a moral, ethical, public social sense.

Let me give a brief gloss on each of these and then deal with them in some more detail.

First: English as a carrier of definitions of culture. Apart from the more general issue of definitions of culture, here questions of value are at issue: the values of different cultural groups in a society. What are the histories of the different groups in this society? How is power distributed between them at the moment? How could or should that be changed? What are the valued texts of a particular group? What are its valued forms of communication? What are its valued forms of language? This picture changes when we turn to considerations of a social kind: now questions of *relative* value arise, the value of one culture ranged relative to that of another; and so, cultural value as such is replaced by *structures of evaluation*. Here the curriculum at once becomes political: when the values of this group are treated by one group as permanently and inherently less valuable than the values of that other social or ethnic group. This happens in at least two distinct ways, either when different evaluations are simply asserted, or when the values of one group are presented neutrally, naturally, and obviously, as *the* relevant, important, most highly valued. Usually, and certainly in the latter case, the bases of the evaluation system are concealed, as in the debates around questions of standard English in the curriculum.

The second aspect, English as the carrier of definitions of society – and of the social – deals with issues such as these, through the range of texts which are admitted into the curriculum. What are their relative valuations? From what groups do they come? What are the forms of language which are admitted? Crucial questions here are: is society presented, in the curriculum, as culturally homogeneous or as heterogeneous? as harmonious? as a structure of hierarchically ordered groups? as complex? contradictory? as stable or as dynamically interactive? as naturally so (as just 'human nature'), or as being the one or the other as a result of the operation of power?

When we turn to the issue of English as a medium of communication yet other questions arise. Is the issue a pragmatic/economic one? Is English seen as an economic resource? as a medium of communication, information, of concern to business, commerce, industry much in the same way in which other economic resources (the transport system, for instance) are considered? Here concerns arise with 'clarity' and 'efficiency', and the costs of loss of clarity or efficiency are quantified and calculated as the costs of 'breakdowns in communication', through bad spelling, bad grammar, the inability to write sentences, etc.: so many billions of dollars, pounds, ecus. Alternatively, there is the much more *social* issue of English as the 'lingua franca' of the nation; one of many languages spoken within this society, but the one which serves best not only as a means of communication but also as a means of unification of a nation. And other questions which arise here involve the alternatives to the single homogenising lingua franca: that of a heteroglossic society for instance.

The subject area of English as the place in the overall curriculum where other major modes of communication can – and given the absence of any other places – *must* be raised, is a matter barely discussed. Media Studies, of course, has long existed in English schools and classrooms. However, on the one hand the place of Media Studies in the English curriculum is, as we know, under severe pressure; on the other hand, in Media Studies the form, the *materiality* of the mode of communication, has generally remained relatively backgrounded, with emphasis generally given more to 'content' than to the material form of the medium itself. In a society which is increasingly turning from the verbal to the visual, the latter has barely begun to be researched seriously as a public mode of communication (rather than as a matter of the aesthetic domain). Knowledge of, and competence in, the use of major modes and media of communication will have to become an essential component of the education of all young people. English is, at the moment and for the foreseeable future, the only place in the curriculum where this can happen.

Lastly, English is the only site in the curriculum which can deal with questions of individuality and responsibility in a moral, ethical, public social sense. By this I do not mean the inculcation of narrowly sectarian values of one kind or another, but the examination of issues around notions of the individual: of social structures and of destinies; of notions of citizenship; of humans as having social responsibilities and socially produced characteristics as persons; as well as those traits we usually cover by terms such as individuality. The curriculum as a whole contributes to the development in human beings of what Pierre Bourdieu calls a 'habitus', a set of deeply ingrained dispositions which form a second nature and act as the basis of habitual practices, often no longer available for the individual's inspection. All parts of the curriculum have their part in this, the Mathematics or Science curriculum no less and perhaps as much as the English curriculum. It is, however, only in the English curriculum where these issues are or can be made available for debate.

It is as well to be explicit about this and lay out openly the ethical/moral arguments which attach to differing forms of individuality, as to different forms of sociality. The grounds for choice are then, at the least, clearly articulated and available for further debate and evaluation.

With these issues in mind, I attempt to imagine a future ten, twenty years hence, for that is the period for which our curriculum has to be designed, the period when young people now in schools will be entering into their – we hope – productive social lives.

Let me just recall the four factors which will, I assume, fundamentally shape that future and make it different from our present in absolute fashion: multiculturalism; technological change and development; the economy; transnationalism. What effect does consideration of these factors have on a curriculum for the future? What can we know that each of these will demand from the generation that is now moving into adulthood, during their life-times, or will demand from the five-year-olds now starting in our schools?

To take multiculturalism first. Whatever the official political position taken up at the moment may be, we know that multiculturalism, *inter*culturalism, polyculturalism, will be a more telling fact of all our lives in ten, fifteen, and twenty years' time even than it is now. What kind of English curriculum can prepare children to be *productively intercultural* and polycultural in the society of tomorrow, rather than passively, anxiously or angrily monocultural? What kind of curriculum is needed to produce dispositions, a habitus, which is at ease with cultural difference? Here the place of *texts* is crucial, in two ways: on the one hand texts will have to be selected in such a way that the socially and culturally crucial values and principles can be adequately demonstrated and debated; on the other hand, out of the study of these texts a pedagogically useable theory of text will have to be demonstrable, a theory which is adequate to *all* the demands of the curriculum.

2 A curriculum for innovation

A brief theory of text and language

To assist in thinking about this I propose to use three categories of text:

- the culturally salient text
- the aesthetically valued (and valuable) text
- the mundane text.

Each has a specific function in the curriculum. Each text takes on a quite specific significance, different to that which they have at the moment. In each case my touchstone for inclusion is aptness of purpose for that society two decades hence: aptness both in providing skills, knowledge, understandings and dispositions, sets of values which can lead to productive ways of being in the world. But aptness also in helping to shape a world which offers the characteristics I mentioned earlier.

Let me start with the category of the *culturally salient* text. The culturally salient text is not measured by the criteria of the aesthetically valued text – even in the culture in which it originates. It is measured not against criteria of beauty but against criteria of *significance*: what significance does this text have in its own cultural domain; what significance can or perhaps should it have, therefore, for members of other cultural groups in this multicultural society? What are the features and characteristics which give it salience in its culture of origin and therefore lend it particular force and significance as a means of understanding that cultural group, in the society of which it is a part? Aesthetically valuable texts may be among these: but that is not a relevant or telling criterion from that point of view.

A shift of this kind, from aesthetic concerns to those of salience, proves essential and liberating, not just within the curriculum but within broader cultural politics. In the context of the latter, it avoids and obviates unproductive debate about 'qualities of writing'; in the context of the former it makes available the materials which are essential to the development of a curriculum for a productively multicultural society.

In this curriculum there will be culturally salient texts which speak of as many of the cultural groups in the society as is pedagogically sound; but in any case, a collection of texts from a range of cultural groups sufficient to establish, on the one hand, crucial points about ways of reading these texts, and to be able to establish a multicultural habitus through the study, among other things, of such texts and to illustrate, on the other hand, the kinds of concerns, the contents of which are central to the concerns of cultural groups. This collection of texts will include, of course, texts from groups which are, at this point, socially and politically dominant, and that fact will be one aspect of their salience. All of these texts will speak of the histories of their cultures, and, through this point to possible cultural/social futures.

The question of the *aesthetically valued* texts is, in my view, best treated as both a matter of culture and of politics. That is, each cultural group has texts which it treats as valued for aesthetic reasons, and these should be represented in the curriculum. The question of what criteria enter into the definition of aesthetic value is, for me, a social matter – that is, a question of the operation of power over long periods, which has become mystified as the a-historical, a-social, non-power-laden category of *taste*. Hence what is treated as most valued in a society is a reflection of histories of power within one cultural group, and histories of power and domination between cultural groups.

So when Dickens, or Shakespeare, or D.H. Lawrence, are presented as naturally and neutrally as 'what is best' in English Literature, we have a conflation of complex histories of power within one society: so that within élite groups sets of values have become dominant, and the bases of the valuations have been obliterated by being 'naturalised'; and within the society overall, the values of that one group are entrenched as neutral values for *all* groups. A discussion of aesthetically valued texts thus becomes amenable to comparative historical/social analysis, without in any sense diminishing the notion of value, as the value of the aesthetically valued texts, or diminishing the set of cultural values embodied in and accreted around these texts.

In my envisaged curriculum there is a further point in relation to the selection of *kinds* of texts. Although my approach may seem excessively – perhaps depressingly – utilitarian and pragmatic, as it happens I believe strongly in *value*, whether in the aesthetic or in other domains. I believe that there *are* exceptional human achievements; even though I prefer to seek a social and cultural explanation of these. Hence for me the aesthetically valued text has at least a number of functions in the curriculum: to show what a cultural or a social group has, in its histories, regarded as exceptional achievement; to reflect on what it is that has given humans real pleasure; to attempt to relate this to broader social and cultural histories; and lastly, and for me importantly, to make such texts have real effects, via their effects on individual lives, on the broadest social practices.

For this to happen, the characteristics of these texts must be clearly understandable and *relatable* to all other texts in the society. I therefore use a third category, namely that of the *mundane* text. In my envisaged curriculum, the mundane texts must be amenable to contact with and influence by the aesthetically valued text: putting it starkly, the office memo (never mind the *Sun* feature article, or the episode of *EastEnders*) must be amenable to effective influence by features of the Shakespeare play, the nineteenth-century novel, or the Augustan epic. In an effective curriculum all of these texts will be treated within a single, coherent and social-historical theory of text, and not, absolutely not, as discrete, unrelated phenomena.

Let me give a brief example. Mundane texts are overlooked; yet they are the texts which are most telling, in many ways, in our everyday and working lives. They form the bedrock of social and economic life. Without an understanding of the mundane text, and without the confident ability to use it for one's purposes in whatever domain, we cannot be fully effective participants in the economic, social and political life of our group. Moreover, without a deep understanding of the mundane text, we are cut off from a full appreciation of the aesthetically valued text. Perhaps most significantly from the point of view of curriculum, without that understanding it cannot be brought to bear on the everyday. This last point provides the decisive justification for the inclusion of the serious study of the mundane text in the English curriculum – together with the equally serious study of the culturally salient and the aesthetically valued text.

A text, any text, is a microcosm of the social world in which it is made. It encapsulates in an irrefutable form a cultural truth about the individual/s who produced it – be it a film, a letter, any text written in a place of work, a newspaper editorial. Here is an example of the mundane text. To make it safe and harmless, but also to make it strange, I'll choose a text from another culture. It comes from the back of the entrance door to a holiday flat in a small town somewhere on the north coast of New South Wales, in Australia. I saw it in August 1988.

> **Beach House Holiday Units**
> *This unit accommodates 5 persons only. Extra persons will be charged a nightly rate.*
> *Unit to be vacated by 10 a.m. on the day of departure.*
> *Only soft toilet paper to be used in septic toilet & please do not dispose of sanitary pads in toilet.*
> *Garbage bags to be placed out on concrete near barbecue each MONDAY before 7 p.m.*
> *Barbecue is available for your use. Utensils in laundry.*
> *No pets allowed.*
> *No fish to be cleaned on premises.*
> *For safety reasons please turn off heaters & fans when unit is unoccupied.*
> > *Thank-you*
> > *Brian & Norma Denny Prop.*
> *PLEASE DO NOT PUT GARBAGE IN COUNCIL BINS*

On the face of it, this humble text provides nothing more or other than useful and necessary instructions for the holidaymakers who rent this flat for a few days or weeks. Pause over it for a moment, however, and you get a sense of considerable unease on the landlords' part. They know, all at the same time, that their tenants are very likely to be nuisances; careless and abusive of property; deceitful even; yet they are also a necessary evil, paying rent. And somewhere, at the back of my then landlords' minds is the uneasy realisation that yes, these people ought to be treated as visitors, as guests even.

These unpractised constructors of rules and regulations convey, more accurately than any treatise ever could, a deep sense of unease about their place in the world: an unease about tourism, and its role in a changing social, economic and cultural world. They reveal echoes only of acquaintance with the discourses of the enterprise culture which, just a few miles up the coast, produces stunning brochures advertising the new (Japanese-owned) luxury resort. This small text captures with absolute precision that moment when an older cultural form of the world – exemplified by English postcard seaside landladies of the 1930s and 1940s – is about to be swept away, to be replaced by the polished world of holidays as commodities, and holidaymakers as customers or clients, a world dominated by the brilliantly edged discourses of contemporary advertising and marketing.

The unease of this text betrays its makers' lack of knowledge about the nature of this change, and about this world. It betrays an inability to control the formal resources which would permit them to make a different text, which would respond to that change with full understanding, either rejecting the glib new world, or embracing it, or perhaps forging some position that they could feel comfortable about.

As a teacher, this mundane text allows me to talk about the uses of language in response to social demands, and in attempts at shaping the social world in response to clearly understood wishes. It allows me to engage in a discussion about change, the pace of change, and the linguistic resources – a full knowledge of grammar, a deep understanding of text and the forms of texts – that will be essential for my students to be able to write the text that they will both need and wish to write in a time of perplexing uncertainties.

But this text also speaks of social and cultural values: of the kinds of cultural and economic shifts that have turned landlords into hosts and tenants into guests (or which allow the manager of the underground station I use every day to address me as 'one of my customers' when I stubbornly want to see myself as a passenger). Out of an understanding of this text can come productively useable knowledge about language – securely founded on knowledge of grammar of a *relevant* kind – about change and how to respond productively, innovatively, and agentively to change. And yes, out of this text can come a deep understanding of the history of a culture – in this instance working-class cultures of the 1930s, 1940s and 1950s and of their contemporary counterparts.

But out of this text can come another realisation, at least as important in giving students a textual theory which can make *them* truly productive users of their language. Consider this other text below. It is separated from the one just above by twenty years and by 14,000 miles. It comes from Norwich, in England, in 1974.

Swimming club rules

1. *Parents must accompany and take responsibility for their children at all times, unless the child is in the water in an instructed class. Note - In most cases this will mean one adult enrolling with one child, or, if they so wish one adult with more than one child provided it is understood they are responsible for them.*

2. *Being absent for more than three consecutive sessions without explanation to the membership secretary means automatic expulsion.*

3. *No outside shoes will be worn when in the pool area.*

4. *Please respect the facilities and equipment, and take particular care with untrained children.*

5. *The age limits of the club are six months to eight years. For the six to eight years old instruction will be provided. Children may remain members for the completed term in which their eighth birthday falls.*

6. *There must be no more than twenty-four bodies in the pool at any one time.*

7. *Membership cards must always be carried and shown on request.*

The similarities between the two texts are, to me, astonishing: the content is different, even though certain kinds of anxieties are common to both – whether about fish or sanitary pads or untrained children – as are certain fears of lawlessness – whether about the wearing of improper shoes or about the twenty-fifth body in the pool, or about 'extra persons' or 'no pets'.

But what is stunningly similar is the social uncertainty, the unsureness about how to represent the relations between the writers and the readers, in their social roles. Should these be clear and unambiguous rules, authoritative, perhaps authoritarian, or should they be relatively friendly demands or statements?

The reasons for this fundamental problem of 'address' are the same in both cases: a confusion about social relations which does not permit a clear generic form (rules or regulations, or 'invitations', or information) to emerge. In the case of the swimming club rules, the situation was one where a group of young mums who knew each other well 'socially', had got together to form a babies' swimming club. Consequently, their relations as friends interfered with their other set of relations as rule-makers.

This approach to text gives a student insight into the reasons for the existence of (generic) forms of a text, and at the same time equips her or him with knowledge, principles and skills on the basis of which they can understand their own text-making, and shape that successfully to their ends.

However, this has not answered the point about the connection between the mundane text, and the aesthetically valued text. Let me give the briefest example of what I have in mind, within an overarching textual theory which accommodates texts of all kinds, and does not separate the mundane from the aesthetic.

Take the opening lines of Shakespeare's *King Lear*. On stage are Kent and Gloucester, both Earls.

	Act I Scene I
Kent:	*I thought the King had more affected the Duke of Albany than Cornwall.*
Gloucester:	*It did always seem so to us; but now in the division of the Kingdom, it appears not which of the Dukes he values most; for equalities are so weighed that curiosity in neither can make choice of either's moiety.*
Kent:	*Is not this your son, my lord?*
Gloucester:	*His breeding, sir, hath been at my charge. I have so often blushed to acknowledge him that now I am brazed to it.*
Kent:	*I cannot conceive you.*
Gloucester:	*Sir, this young fellow's mother could: whereupon she grew round-wombed, and had indeed, sir, a son for her cradle ere she had a husband for her bed. Do you smell a fault?*
Kent:	*I cannot wish the fault undone, the issue of it being so proper.*
Gloucester:	*But, I have a son, sir, by order of law, some year elder than this, who yet is no dearer in my account: though this knave came something saucily into the world before he was sent for, yet was his mother fair; there was good sport at his making, and the whoreson must be acknowledged. – Do you know this noble gentleman, Edmund?*

Gloucester uses the 'royal plural': *we, us* – in the seventeenth century, the pronoun used by the powerful of themselves or to each other to signal power rather than solidarity. Kent uses the singular form *I, my*: the form used by the powerful to signal solidarity (and absence of power), and used to intimate others of the same rank or downward to the lower orders. Shakespeare establishes for the audience, through this minute but precise device, an immediate distinction between the two Earls: one plain and straightforward, the other pompous and a buffoon. It also allows him to deflate Gloucester, for when his bastard son Edmund comes on stage, Gloucester, embarrassed by his past misdemeanour, starts to use the singular form of himself: his pomposity is pricked.

An unevenness, a fluctuation, an unease in the text – here deliberately produced – signals exactly the same meaning as in the earlier examples, even if at a very general, abstract level – namely a shiftingness, an uneasiness about social relations.

This is a slight example, admittedly, though I think the point is not. It will allow a connection, once the principle is recognised, of texts across centuries, as here, and enable students to imagine themselves as manipulators of these very devices.

Such a theory of text presupposes an explicitness of the English curriculum about matters of language form, language use – in the widest senses – which is not available in English curricula at the moment, either to students or to many of their teachers. It includes an explicitness about practices of writing and reading. Out of such an explicit curriculum constituted not only around a selection of texts, but, importantly, constituted around means of reading – comes the possibility of productive use of the kind and range of texts I have indicated. It encompasses, in its scope, all the questions around language: language use, change and development. A curriculum which deals adequately with this range of texts is also a curriculum which develops essential practices (and theories) of reading and of writing.

Of course, such a theory and such practices rest on an understanding of a *whole text*, with an understanding of the complex contexts of its production and of its usual contexts of reading/reception in considerable detail. This will demand of the English curriculum a fully and explicitly developed social and cultural theory of text, within which a linguistic theory of text is one component. Crucially for both this socio-cultural theory and for the linguistic theory, text has to be seen as the product of many voices, from many places in society: an object with a multiple producership and a multiple readership. Clearly, a text has, therefore, many readings, though not, as in some commonsense accounts, an unconstrained set of readings – 'a text means just what I want it to mean'; but a set of readings constrained on the one hand by its conditions of production, and the forms which encode these in the text, and, on the other hand, by its conditions of reception, and the forms, usually unseen, which are produced in a reader's readings.

In moving to a brief exemplification of such a form of reading I will highlight one further aspect of a reading theory and of reading practices which seems to me foundational, but not usually focused on. It arises from the sketch I have outlined so far, and it concerns the question of the boundaries of the text to be read.

My example (overleaf) is a page from the *Daily Express*.

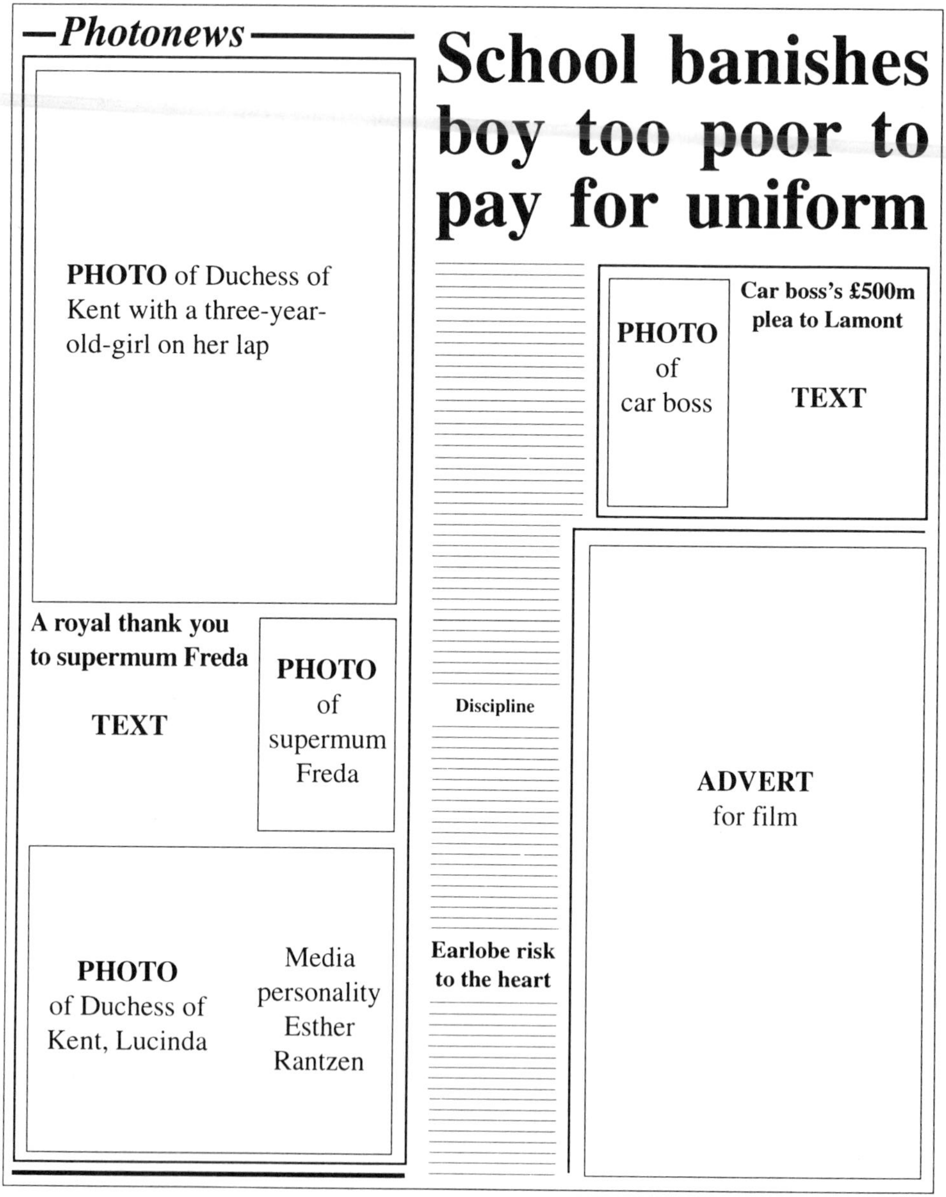

—*Photonews*—

School banishes boy too poor to pay for uniform

PHOTO of Duchess of Kent with a three-year-old-girl on her lap

A royal thank you to supermum Freda

TEXT

PHOTO of supermum Freda

Discipline

PHOTO of Duchess of Kent, Lucinda

Media personality Esther Rantzen

Earlobe risk to the heart

PHOTO of car boss

Car boss's £500m plea to Lamont

TEXT

ADVERT for film

Figure 3: Sample page from the Daily Express

It has several articles, the main ones being the 'Photonews' article, and the article about the boy whose parents were too poor to buy a uniform, which I'll call the 'Poverty' article. The question is, how do we read, let's say, the 'Poverty' article? On the face of it, its boundaries are clearly marked, and so a reading should be perfectly possible which attends to this article alone. Here is most of this text:

> *A schoolboy was taught in a class on his own because his parents could not afford a uniform, it was revealed yesterday.*
>
> *The 13-year-old was separated from classmates for several weeks, a community advice organisation said. His misery only ended when his friends found enough jumble in an Oxfam shop for a make-shift uniform.*
>
> *'It is the worst case of this kind we have seen,' said Nichola Simpson, head of policy at the National Association of Citizens Advice Bureaux.*
>
> *'It was very distressing for a boy so young. And he missed out educationally. Children should not suffer like that, especially because they cannot afford a uniform. It was a very hard-hearted thing to do.'*
>
> *The incident happened in the East Midlands earlier this year when the boy's family moved into the area.*
>
> *His parents were on income support, but education chiefs told them they did not qualify for a grant because their son moved schools mid-term.*
>
> *The case was revealed by the association in a report on uniforms.*
>
> *It said many poor children were suffering at school because local bureaucrats are not helping them pay for uniforms.*
>
> *Many parents on benefits or low incomes were not receiving grants, which are discretionary.*
>
> *The news comes as many schools return to uniforms in a bid to make pupils more presentable and disciplined.*
>
> *But the NACAB found local authority provision for uniform and clothing grants was tending to 'wither away'.*
>
> (*Daily Express*, 3 May 1991)

However, within it there are, as a closer reading reveals, several accounts of poverty. One says broadly that poverty is caused by the heartlessness and inefficiencies of teachers, and of educational and local authority bureaucrats. Just some examples of this are: 'School banishes boy. . . ' 'The 13-year-old was separated from classmates [by?]'; 'It was a very hard-hearted thing to do'; 'education chiefs told them they did not qualify'; 'local bureaucrats are not helping them'; etc.

Another account, not so strongly marked (and expressed more through syntactic forms than through overt content), suggests that poverty is a state you're in, without any particular cause, or remedy. 'His misery only ended'; 'It was very distressing'; 'The incident happened'; 'His parents were on income support'; 'local authority provision . . . was tending to wither away'. In all these examples the action seems uncaused; it simply *is*, or happens; in 'provision . . . wither away', it is clear to see that an ideologically motivated selection has been made here to obscure or deny agency. Yet another reading suggests that poverty is within the control of the poor: both 'being able *to buy* a uniform', and '*affording* a uniform', look, on the surface, like ordinary transitive verbs, and transitive verbs, as we know, express actions which are under the control of the actor who performs this action, expressed by the subject-noun. For instance, in *'The postman delivered the letter', the postman* is the grammatical subject, and names the actor who is responsible for the process of *delivering* (and of its effects).

The text, I hope it is clear, contains a number of different accounts of poverty, and not a single, coherent account. The different accounts originate from distinctly different social positions. In part, a strong linguistic theory of text is as essential a prerequisite for this reading, as is a strong cultural–social theory: or rather, what is needed is a theory of texts in which the two are not distinguished. In other words, the appropriate theory of text should allow us to talk about what seem to be merely formal properties of the text – the use of transitive or intransitive verb types for instance – and to account for these in terms of the social histories, places, and motivations of the makers of texts: 'this intransitive verb is here because the makers of the text did not wish to focus on or mention agency'.

This, however, is not the end of the story for me. If it is the case that the text within the boundaries as indicated on the page (the 'Poverty' text) already has a number of different 'reading positions' coded in its syntax, positions from which different kinds of readers could comfortably read this text, it is also the case that the texts with which it appears on the page add further possibilities of understanding to its account of poverty. Or, to be more precise, the co-texts on this page tend in a direction which encourage one reading more than others, which make one reading more plausible than the others. The 'Photonews' article shows how the state (in the guise of a member of the royal family, of a privatised enterprise, and of the media) cares for those who care; the 'Car boss plea' article shows that hardship is widespread, not confined only to 'the poor'; and so on.

In other words, for anyone who reads more than just the one article on this page, the explanations provided by that *one* article are shifted, narrowed, altered by reading the others. The question arises, therefore, as to what, for that reader (not, after all, an unusual or subversive reader) the text *is*? what the boundaries of the text are? If the meanings of one article are significantly shaped by the entirely ordinary practice of reading other, co-present articles, then the boundary of the text-to-be-read actually may be the page; or it may be a series of articles in this paper; or in all the media, over a particular period.

The question touches on two issues: what is our theory of reading, and what reading practices follow?; and, can a reliance on language alone produce an adequate theory of text, or of reading? In my view text is always a social/cultural product; and any plausible account of a text therefore has to be a social/cultural explanation, of which a strong linguistic account is an essential component. Many currently favoured theories of reading focus on narrow, entirely formalistic aspects of reading; decoding, in effect, only one of the many codes which are in play. Certain forms of 'phonics' are an instance of this. On the other side are equally problematic theories of reading which operate, in effect, without any attention to form. Their effects are no less disabling.

The problem is reinforced by authoritarian pedagogies, which insist on strict policing of boundaries; indeed, there is a correlation between the strictness of boundary-maintenance – what can be brought into relevance in a reading, or who decides the boundaries of the unit to be read – and a restriction on the *size* of the unit around which the boundaries are drawn, so that one might be tempted to establish a rule to the effect that tightness of boundary control, and the size of the unit which is bounded, stand in an inverse relation to the effort spent on enforcing control. That is, the greater the effort to exert control and the stricter the policing, the smaller the unit. A focus on letter/sound correlation as a central aspect of reading is an example. The rule operates, I suggest, equally well in the opposite direction: the less effort that is expended in control, the less the policing, the larger the unit to be read – or the range of elements that can be drawn into a reading. Certain 'reading for meaning' approaches are examples.

This is a domain where theory in its normal sense is crosscut by issues which are entirely political; and it is as well to recognise that fact. The questions to put – to parents, to politicians, teachers, business people, to all those interested in reading theory – are these: what is it you wish to solve? what is it you wish to achieve? Is the problem you wish to deal with a curricular/pedagogic one, or is it a political, ideological one? Are you interested in your child learning to read? or are you interested in your child learning to stay within boundaries?

In raising the question of the boundaries of text and therefore of the boundaries of reading, a further issue arises, which takes us beyond another crucial boundary, namely that of language. In suggesting that a reader might read more than one 'article' together, I glossed over the question of what might determine first, which article is read first, and second, whether, if more than one article is read, we can speculate about the order of reading, and the effect of that. However, in doing so, we have to pass across the boundary between two media of expression, from the written, linguistic, to the visual. In the two questions of what is read first? and what is the order in which the articles are read? we have moved to drawing in another medium, the visual medium, structured both through the rule-system of layout which might simply place two written texts together on a page in a particular order; and by readers' preferences between the linguistic and the visual. In doing so, we have moved from a theory of text which is purely verbal, to a theory of text which treats the page as a visual unit, and we have moved from linguistics to semiotics.

The page, as a unit of visual composition, offers particular possibilities of reading. On the one hand, the page-editor uses layout to construct a preferred 'reading path', a suggestion to readers about the order or sequence in which they might read the page – through bold headlines, images, and the positioning of items on the page (e.g. centrality; use of the possibilities of a left to right reading path; and top vs bottom structures). As with the construction of other suggested reading paths or reading positions, a reader will either fall in with this preferred structure or resist it. For instance, a reader oriented to language as the most important medium may be most attracted by the bold headline; another reader, more attracted by the visual medium, may read the 'Photonews' story first; yet another reader may have a preference for reading from left to right. The reading-path is therefore neither entirely determined by the makers of the page – though they do provide a structure which has effects; nor is it accidental, or the result of whim: it is the effect of personal/cultural history and disposition. These are culturally produced preferences, and habitual readers of a particular newspaper are likely to become influenced – and 'trained' – by a paper's practices, and therefore more accustomed to one form of reading than another.

An expansion of the boundaries of the text-to-be-read entails a shift from consideration within one medium, that of language, to a consideration of the page as a visual unit, in which language is now simply an element. Once that move has been made, we have to attempt to understand a distinctly different medium to that of language, the visual, whether in the form of layout, or of images, or both, in its own specific terms.

This is now all the more urgent as there is a strongly marked shift from the linguistic to the visual in many areas of public communication. The reasons for that shift in the landscape of public communication are complex; they are easier to illustrate than to explain. A favoured explanation, in as far as explanations of this phenomenon are attempted, is that of the effects of technology. The story goes something like this: 'improvements in technology make it easier to use images, and make it possible to use colour'. As with most explanations which make technology causal, this seems to me too superficial. The *Frankfurter Allgemeine* has, it must be assumed, the same technological resources available to it as *The Sun*, yet the former uses neither colour nor images on its front page. There are deeper causes at work, enormously significant changes for anyone involved in education to understand. In its most general form one might say that this is about a change in the public role of written language, which seems, for some papers (though not for the *Frankfurter Allgemeine*) no longer unproblematically available as a reliable means of public communication.

Implied in this is a change in the envisaged reader: away from the reader who is prepared to devote detailed, analytical, sustained attention to written language (the reader of the *Frankfurter Allgemeine*, with a quite specific rationality) towards the reader who expects to obtain information more immediately, more rapidly, perhaps more impressionistically, through visual modes (images, bold headlines), who expects to be entertained (hence the use of colour), who does not expect to spend time in reading with attention and concentration (hence the decrease in the amount of verbal text). It is important to insist that these are implications, *not* descriptions of actual readers. There may be readers who study images with the same detailed, analytical attention as many readers devote to written text; just as there are readers of written text who read impressionistically.

For me there are a number of explanations. One of the most plausible lies in far-reaching social changes, of which multiculturalism, and the deep uncertainties produced by it in so many areas of social life, may be a fundamentally significant one; and equally far-reaching – and in many ways connected – changes in the global economy may be another. The globalisation of mass-media makes the visual a seemingly more accessible medium, certainly more accessible than any particular language. The effects of these for human subjects, and of a disposition of various kinds, comes about because of the representational resources which are made available to members of cultural and social groups. The front page of *The Sun* makes available one set of representational resources and does so in particular configurations: usually one large image, and a single 'story' connected to the image with hugely bold headlines (expressed as a proportion of the total page). The (semiotic) import is something like this: on the front page, the page which tells you what it is most important to know today, we give you, in immediately accessible and pleasurable form (the image, the bold headline, the minute amount of linguistic text, colour) the single (or the two) most important event(s) today. This highly abstract message, insistently put forward day after day after day, produces a reading practice which in its turn engenders dispositions which rely both on particular kinds of representational resources, and on particular configurations of these: the visual as dominant, relying on immediate accessibility and on pleasurability; while the verbal is subordinated, and what has so far been seen as the 'rational' means of gaining information is made marginal.

This habitus is produced, I wish to suggest, by real social and economic factors; it is given continuous, insistent expression through the implicit projection of a particular kind of reader: not only in *The Sun*, nor only in advertisements, but in government publications – have a look at the *Parents' Charter*; and it appears in places where *I* certainly would not have expected it – have a look at a university prospectus, and not only those of the 'newer' universities! I ask myself, 'What does it mean when a university addresses those who will be its students in this form?' I think it signals a loss of nerve about the values of the university – and has repercussions about how it can deal with the students once they get there.

I have in mind as I write this the prospectus of a well-established civic university, somewhere in Central England; the contents pages consist almost entirely of small, colourful, photographic images, about twenty of them. Language is remarkable by its near absence: you have to hunt to find verbal labels for the different sections of the prospectus.

This is the context in which we have to set our own efforts in relation to literacy; though it is also the context in which the political polemic around literacy has to be understood. The question for me, going back to the principles I mentioned at the beginning, is about representational resources: what representational resources does the curriculum need to make available to all students, so that they have a real possibility of self-directed action, whether as readers or as writers, in their society. The reader that I envisage will understand, on the one hand, that the notion of 'reader-friendliness' (whether used by *The Sun* or by a university) is the guise under which much more serious social, political and ideological work is being done, and is one cover for significant shifts in social arrangements which may be anything but friendly to her or to him. This reader will understand that in the totality of representational resources which the paper uses and presents, and in their characteristic configuration, s/he is addressed as a particular kind of social being. But this kind of reader will also understand both that there are deep and long-term changes taking place here, which it is essential to understand; and that their form offers possibilities and resources which must be fully available for their own use as makers of texts.

Of course, in all this there are fairly direct links to the economy and to technology. The shift from information to entertainment changes me from reader to consumer, and is itself linked to, and expressive of, fundamental shifts in the economy – however much this shift has been further amplified; and it is skewed by sets of ideologies which are derivative of this change: 'marketisation', 'consumerisation,' and the wholesale invasion of everyday language by the discourses of 'economic rationalism'.

If this sounds too recognisably like the usual Jeremiad about traditional modes of communication – the decline of standards; loss of values; the end of civilisation as we knew and loved it; etc. – let me issue a corrective. I am much more interested in understanding this change than in bewailing it: yes, on the one hand understanding what may be *lost* if we move from lettered representation – literacy – to representation through images. I am at least equally interested in understanding the possibilities of the newer modes: what do *they* make possible, what potentials do *they* open up, what forms of individuality and sociality are implied in them? Chinese cultures have, seemingly, managed to do extremely well for several thousand years, with a representational system based on images. 'Tests show', as they say, that young Chinese massively outclass those whose major representational system is alphabetic, in visual analytic ability. If the new information-based economies will need visual analysis as a fundamental requirement, perhaps we had better move with the greatest speed in that direction.

The links to technology are in part obvious: certain changes in technology – electronic text and data processing and reproduction, image and colour reproduction, layout practices – are all making this shift so much more possible. But the connection of the English curriculum to technology has a more profound aspect in relation to a theory of text. The technologies of communication, reproduction, and of *processing* are not only affecting the relative significance of different media, they are also crucially implicated in a speeding up of the dissolution of the boundaries of generic form, speeding up of rates of generic change, and at the same time, paradoxically, productive of a likelihood of conformities to an extent we have not so far known.

Let me point to two areas: forms of writing have had a *relative* stability over the last forty years or so, even though forms of written text, genres, have been affected and changed by social changes. Electronic media are likely to bring radical changes. If writing has, in our experience, been shaped (in its grammar/syntax as much as in its generic form) by the temporal and physical distance between the writer and the addressee – in contradistinction to speech – e-mail now makes possible a hitherto impossible situation where a writer is physically distant from and yet in the communicational presence of the reader (a situation previously made possible in the realm of speech, through the telephone). This will have fundamental effects on the grammar/syntax and the textual forms of writing.

As my other example of a paradoxical kind, consider the effects of developments I mentioned before, in word processing, including speech-recognition technologies, on English as a world language. These depend on hardware and on software as I pointed out. Developments in the latter will depend on advances in parsing programmes, themselves of course dependent on developments in grammatical theories. On the one hand the kind of grammatical theory adopted, and on the other hand the form of English chosen, will together determine the kind of English which will be 'recognisable' to the technology. Given that the hardware and the programmes are likely in the medium term to be concentrated in the ownership of a very few transnational companies, the effects on English as an international language are not difficult to imagine. Because of the tight links of the British economy into transnational capital and the global economy, these effects will be transmitted into the use of English in Britain. Conformity will be established in certain domains on a global level. In this context, a productive knowledge of essential representational resources, established through a broad, representative range of culturally and socially salient texts, is an absolute prerequisite.

I mentioned earlier that my aim at this stage is to begin to establish an agenda of principles which can be publicly debated, and, I hope, even if not eventually publicly agreed, then at least thoroughly established in public consciousness. I wish to oppose principles designed for the further polarisation of this society and, as its best hope offered at the moment, nothing beyond the competent management of decline and, through that, the condemnation of the majority of children now in school to ever bleaker lives, a future of hopeless despair. I am interested in principles which build on the historical and social strengths of Britain over the last three centuries, and use the tremendous new resources of a multicultural Britain, which can be used to construct a productive tomorrow. My aim most immediately is to develop a project to set against the savagely destructive intents of the presently dominant one: to deploy energies and imagination around that project.

Of course, many elements of the present National Curriculum will be present in that agenda; and it will contain much of what is the taken-for-granted practice of English teachers. In some, for me, crucial respects, it will go beyond these. Above all it is a project which in this period of deliberately wrought wreckage allows us to develop an Utopian vision and to mobilise the support of those who can imagine a different society around it.

Textual theory in curriculum practice

At this point it may be useful to exemplify my textual theory in some detail, with an eye on curriculum application. I will take the *holiday units* text (see page 37) as my example. There are six points I will make though I won't devote equal space to each:

1. Text is constructed by social individuals in their social world, and text reconstructs that world in its turn.
2. Text is made using both social resources and linguistic resources, and these two are intensely interrelated.
3. Texts are produced by social individuals with particular histories, dispositions, social places, and texts imply particular kinds of readers.

4. Textual *theories* imply particular kinds of readers.
5. Texts as social constructs, exist in the form of particular genres, or as mixed genres.
6. Texts have the closest interconnection with the cultural contexts in which they are produced.

To take them in turn.

1. As I mentioned when I introduced this text earlier, it arises out of a set of contradictory, confused social relations (as does the babies' swimming club text). Norma and Brian are (seaside) landlady and landlord – although the Australian version of that role is clearly different to that which is still familiar from English seaside postcards. Nevertheless, the affinities are clear. As (temporary) landlords they are in a legal relation with 'tenants', in which, on the whole, landlords have rights and tenants have duties, landlords have power and tenants do not. Evidence of this relation is everywhere present in this little text – largely in the various forms of command: 'Unit to be vacated by 10 a.m.'; 'Only soft toilet paper to be used'; 'No pets allowed'; 'No fish to be cleaned'; etc. Norma and Brian prefer not to use imperatives here (which is the 'usual', 'normal' syntactic form of command) except for the commands about sanitary pads, fans and heaters, and the last command 'Do not put garbage in council bins'; but they are all 'softened' by 'Please'. Presumably they felt insufficiently powerful or simply 'uneasy' to use direct imperatives; and so declaratives (the 'normal' syntactic form for statements) are used by them instead. Syntactically speaking, their meaning is: 'We're just telling you' and not: 'We're ordering you to'.

The – probably unintended – consequence of using declaratives as commands is that *all* declaratives in this text take on an air of command: I know that 'This unit accommodates 5 persons only' means 'Do not bring six people'; but I'm also beginning to feel that 'Barbecue is available for your use' may actually mean 'Use the b . . . barbecue!'

The relation of host and guest here is more by implication perhaps than in what is actually written. The 'Barbecue is available for your use. Utensils in laundry' are really the only overt signs of this relation, except for indirect signs, which I have already mentioned, namely that imperatives seem to be used only where really serious issues – blocked toilets, burned down flats, and trouble with the Council – are threatening.

But the text also constructs a social world: it defines, from the moment I read it, who I am (assumed) to be, and the relation between myself and my – even temporary –landlords. Its effects reach further, in that I am now worried about any sixth person who threatens to stay beyond 6 p.m., and about the other members of my party, who might at any moment infringe any of these rules. Further than this, the text projects an image of a social world within a larger world, in which not many miles from these holiday units a brand new Japanese-owned and run holiday resort has opened, which addresses holidaymakers in an entirely different fashion: within the new discourses of tourism as a commodity, and holidaymakers as guests, and as valued customers/ clients. In other words, I now read this text, which fifteen years ago was unremarkable, in the context of a changed social and discursive world. That world has not only produced the *new* texts of tourism, it has made *me* different: elsewhere along this coast I can now demand to be treated in a different way to that implied by this notice, and it is *that* as much as anything else that makes me a different, a critical, reader of this text.

This approach to text places social considerations to the fore, it alerts students to that constructedness, and to its effects. It makes possible a quite informed mode of teaching text, one that students can relate to their immediate experience.

2. My second point really follows from this. Norma's and Brian's difficulty is both a social and a linguistic one. As far as the latter is concerned I assume that they are unpractised writers of this sort of text: they do not have the necessary resources, so that an existing social awkwardness is intensified by a linguistic one. At the same time, it may well be the case that even if they could produce a different text they would not want to do so – they do not have the wish, or the social (and cultural and personal) resources to transform this situation by transforming themselves. Here too, there is a fundamental point for the curriculum: linguistic form always directly entails social meanings; they are never separable, *pace* the assumptions of common-sense that form and meaning are arbitrarily connected.

3. My third point has been made, though it is important to be aware of it precisely: the historical 'datedness' of this text is an inevitable characteristic of all texts. Texts are made, and encode the particular kinds of social relations of *now*, and imply particular kinds of participants – writers, readers, and others; once made, the inevitable dynamic of the social world has already moved things on. The effect of the text is a conservative one; to slow down the dynamic of social change: this little text, written some years before I saw it, judging by the faded card on which it appeared, fixes or at least attempts to fix social relations; it wants me to be *now* as I might have been fifteen years ago. Texts precisely encode a situation now – who the writer thinks I am, who I think my readers are, how we relate – and texts become, immediately, models of that relation projected and active into the future.

That, of course, among many others, is one reason why canonical texts have become or have been made canonical, and why they invite such intense debate about their canonical status. Texts teach us, they provide us with models of the cultural and social world; of who we might be in that world. Considerations such as these point forward to a concern I explore below, namely about the kinds of texts and contents we bring into this curriculum which we will need in order to allow young people to make for themselves the resources to be able to deal with difference of all kinds productively, and as a source of innovation.

4. This connection with 'contents' is significant, because it provides one of the anchoring and defining aspects of the curriculum: what resources, of what kinds, we will make available to children in schools, which is my fourth point. My exceedingly mundane text implies, by its hypothesised inclusion in my curriculum, a focus of a particular kind – a focus not on the élite and its texts, but a focus precisely on the significance of understanding the everyday, a focus away from the English curriculum based on the aesthetic (and historical etc.) concerns of the élite and its texts, and on the cultural, social, pragmatic concerns of the majority of children in schools; not, I hasten to say, in order to exclude the aesthetic, but in order to place it productively in the full range of texts in a society. If I am keen to improve the quality of notices of this kind, or of office-memos, or of government reports – or, a more significant aim, to enable young men and women to understand the cultural and social principles of their constitution, then I need a theory which makes it completely usual to place the aesthetically valued text right next to the mundane text and discuss them in the same theoretical framework, and as being, importantly, of the same order of significance.

That of itself already implies a certain pedagogy; the focus on the social contingency of the textual, generic form of this text as of all texts, and of its character (again as of *all* texts in different ways and to different degrees) as a *mixed genre* (rule, information, and invitation), presupposes a relatively open, non-authoritarian mode of teaching as essential and as normal.

5. This brings me to the question of genre. However awkwardly it does so, this text reminds us of other texts of a similar kind – the babies' swimming club text, for instance, or of literally hundreds of notices in sports clubs, hotel rooms, etc. If it is the case that we recognise texts of this kind (however awkwardly produced), it must be the case that they have a relative repeatability and stability, which derives from the relative stabilities of social arrangements. I imagine that in a few years' time texts of this kind will no longer be seen – an effect not of textual changes alone or even predominantly, but an effect of far-reaching social changes.

For me, the absolutely central point for the curriculum is this: in a multicultural society, the social and cultural assumptions which are central in the making of text, cannot be assumed to be shared, and known, by all children. Hence the curriculum must make those knowledges which are central to their success available, and do so explicitly.

6. The sixth and last point by now hardly needs further elucidation. I will simply say that this humdrum, exceedingly mundane text can reveal, or be made to reveal, as much about culture, society, power, identity, as many other seemingly more 'elevated' texts. This issue is important now and will probably be more so in the future. A major point pedagogically is that of textual theory, and how it places students in their relation to the texts of others, whether of the élite, or of cultural others or indeed the texts of their own group. A further point is that with an increasing shift in the curriculum – inevitably and perhaps necessarily – towards *modes of analysis as the new content* – we need to be able to see methodology not simply as a sterile and bleak matter of the application, mindlessly, of formalisms, but as elucidating cultural meanings. The issue of value needs, I believe, to move decisively back into the centre of concerns of the curriculum: but this time, in the intra- and internationally pluricultural world, the principles of valuation will need to be open and explicit, rather than implicit as they have been.

Ways of thinking and forms of representation

Every now and then our attention is drawn to an argument between a famous film-director and an equally famous novelist over the adaptation of a novel into a film. Both claim that the other doesn't understand what is at issue – the truth of the novel, or of the film.

Some of these involve cases where the novelist had been asked to produce the script – usually not to the director's liking. What is at issue in these quarrels is a fundamental matter, which is usually invoked in some form or another, but which is never fully articulated. It is the plain fact that two distinct modes of representation (or multiple modes) are involved, between which there can be no simple transduction. Different media have distinct potentials of expression and representation and 'translations' between them are at best approximations. Any one mode of representation has certain potentials and certain limitations. The verbal medium, speech particularly, is bound by the logic of sequence: one thing has to be said after another, quite simply. That imposes limitations when seen from the point of view of the visual – which can represent complex structures at once. But it means that a particularly suitable mode of expression for time-based media, such as speech (or film, or dance, or gesture) is the narrative: so much so that we have come to believe – and this forms a common-sense in much English teaching – that narrative is the natural form, or an essential form, somehow characteristic, of human thought.

Narrative *is* a basic form, due to the fact that speech, with its logic of sequence, is an ubiquitous human form of communication, and that human practices occur in sequence, over time, in the natural punctuations of days, years, lives. The newly re-introduced visual forms of electronic technologies may have quite different characteristics; those of spatial rather than of temporal organisation for instance, or that of the web-like organisation of the data-base.

As far as the curriculum for the future is concerned a number of things are essential here. First and foremost, we need to be careful not to import present common-sense into that future unexamined; for instance, that family of ideas which equates language and thought. Secondly, we need to be aware of the potential, and limitations, of each medium. And if texts are becoming more intensely multimodal, we need to understand that the production or reading of a text will involve distinctly different perceptual, cognitive and affective modes all at the same time. Thirdly, it is the case that we know very little indeed about the transductive work done by the brain – which allows us to *tell* someone, in language, what a picture is like; or enables others to produce a visual representation from a verbal text. Consider, as an example, the complex set of links between the images in Figure 4, (see page 58) and the activities which I suspect were involved in producing Figure 5 (see page 59).

Figure 4 reproduces six images produced by a five-year-old boy, on small square pages from a note-pad. After he had drawn them he was spotted by one of his parents arranging them in pairs on the floor in the hallway of their house. When asked what he was doing he gave the explanation which is reproduced in the caption to each pair of images. Some weeks later, at the end of his school term, he brought home some of his school-books, one of which contained the page reproduced here as Figure 5. It had been done, at school, several weeks before the images in Figure 4. I am interested in the complex series of transductions which the child performed, starting with his teacher's initial (verbal) instructions and explanations, to the cognitive and physical/*manual* act of classification and joining of the images on the stencilled text, to the production of the later images and the much more complex act of classification performed on them without language, I assume; and then the final translation into speech, done for the parent's benefit.

Multimodal texts demand that kind of activity constantly and instantly: at this time, when language is still dominant in terms of our cultural valuations and assumptions, explanations are largely given in language: it acts as the universal semiotic solvent. (Exceptions to this are, for instance, 'demonstrations', where I *show* someone how to get somewhere, or do something.) There is no reason why this should or will remain the case. We may well, in the future, expect to be asked to provide visual summaries of extensive slabs of verbal text: indeed, in some domains that is already the case, as in the largely diagrammatic summary report for the Board of Directors, or the largely visual briefing for a group, relying on graphed representations of various kinds. If my hypothesis about the needs of information-handling are correct, then this will become the common, the natural mode.

Children already perform these tasks of transduction: they move between different disciplines in the school curriculum, and they move between the increasingly visual communicational landscape of their out-of-school lives, and the still dominantly verbal one of the school.

'Me and the dog are in life, so they're in the correct order.'

'The flying bomb is in the air and the plane is in the air, so they're in the correct order.'

'The patterns are in the correct order.'

Figure 4: *Visual classification*

Figure 5: *Visual and manual classification*

The promise of the curriculum: contents or resources?

A curriculum is a complex entity, with complex purposes. In more settled periods it may appear that the purpose of schooling is to be one major element of socialisation controlled, in nations such as England, largely by the state. Hence the curriculum is seen as making available kinds of contents which are crucial for the enculturation of the young members of a society, and their socialisation, fitting them for the multiplicity of tasks which need to be undertaken. 'Content' is a word waiting for meaning at the best of times; in times of intensely accelerated change it becomes greatly in need of some more precise meaning.

The problem seems not to be so pressing in other school subjects, and it may be instructive to ask why. In Science, for instance, there is, of course, great debate on what the curriculum should contain and how it should be presented; nevertheless, there is some considerable agreement, namely that it should present a coherent selection of relevant, criterial material from the discipline of Science, suitably mediated for the age-groups at issue. The Science curriculum therefore presents material in some broad domains around which there can be some general agreement in that discipline: physics, chemistry, biology. It presents criterial categories in these areas, organised, in however rudimentary a fashion, in the framework of some at least relatively coherent theory.

The English curriculum has no equivalent discipline standing behind it, and that situation is, if anything, getting more so. No discipline suggests what the contents of the curriculum could or should be, and so the argument tends, in the end, to be settled by sheer political power: nowadays, with little attempts to disguise, a politician decides.

The problem is only in part due to the variety of the often contradictory demands made of the curriculum, which I discussed earlier. It is also caused by an uncertainty about what are the proper demands which should or could be made of it, or which, given its pivotal place in the curriculum and in society, need to be made of it. So if we apply the criteria of the *prospective function* of the curriculum can we get greater clarity? In my view we can.

Let me ask first about present understandings, demands or expectations for 'content', for what the curriculum should deliver. The *explicit* demands tend to be of two kinds, broadly. First is a demand that the contents should allow all children to become integrated in some way into the dominant culture, and, as a sub-part of that demand, a demand that the values of that culture should be produced and transmitted in an integrated, coherent form. This inevitably involves some nostalgic retrospect – the reference to a period when these values are thought to have existed in some agreed, solid form. This is a political, social, ideological demand, dressed up in the guise of the assertion of 'national' cultural values. Second is a demand that the curriculum should serve the economic needs of the country. Here a charge is levelled at curricula that they are not meeting the essential needs and expectations of commerce, industry, and the service industries. The chief culprit here is 'literacy': children, it is said, do not have sufficient literacy skills, that is, they cannot spell, punctuate, form sentences; and cannot communicate effectively in the spoken form of the standard language.

Which of these demands stands up to the requirements of a prospective curriculum? The first set of demands, the 'culturalist' demands, aims to flatten out difference. It aims to achieve its goals largely through the use of canonical texts, as well as through an inculcation of particular modes of reading – 'appreciating' – these texts, as aesthetically valuable, as historically salient. As I have suggested earlier, it is precisely the existence, understanding, appreciation, and productive use of *difference* which is essential as a resource for the future needs of the young people involved, and of the society in which they will live. As I mentioned earlier, texts teach us about the social and cultural world in which they were made: its values, its contents, its structures. A prospective curriculum will need to aim for making students aware of the multiplicity of such cultures and their texts, their contribution and principles of production. So at a cultural level, from a cultural point of view, the curriculum will need to make available salient texts from many cultures. The aim does not have to be exhaustiveness, for plainly it cannot achieve that; however, with an appropriate cultural and social theory of language, children can be given the linguistic, cultural and social resources for an understanding of the constitution of texts, can be brought to understand that all texts always arise out of the structures, values, tensions, of particular cultures and societies.

The first demand is also frequently espoused through demands for a teaching of the standard language. Again this is a political demand, with its exhortation to conformity by all groups to the forms of an élite group. The 'standard' language is the mother tongue of only a small group in this society. At one level the demand is therefore one which assumes that while a small group can speak their mother-tongue in school, in public life, the vast majority must learn a language which is *not* their mother tongue if they wish to participate successfully in the life and values of the public education system, and of public life later on. This demand needs to be examined carefully – both in its present context and for its present effects, and for the curriculum of the future.

Clearly there is no case – although at times there are attempts to make it – that non-standard forms are not communicationally effective. What *is* the case, if we accept that cultural/social groups make their language, is that the resulting language is quite precisely the language which is right for *that* group, communicationally, and in other ways. That also suggests that there are real *differences* between languages (where for these purposes I include dialect in the category of language), corresponding to the differences between the social/ cultural groups. The question is, then, not a linguistic one in the first instance; in the first instance it is a social and political question, namely one which asks which social group is dominant, and which group for *that* reason, and not for linguistic/communicational reasons, can demand that its *language* be dominant.

This leaves, then, for the short term, the question of access: if the language of the dominant group is a means of access to full participation in all aspects of public life, it is the task, I assume, of the educational system, and therefore of the English curriculum, to make the knowledge, this 'content', these resources available to all. In the medium to longer term the situation is different. For one thing, as I mentioned above, the control of dominant forms of English is passing to a new, globally defined group. For another, the communicational landscape is changing with an increasing shift to the visual. And lastly, the social dynamics presently at work are in any case producing changes. As I have pointed out elsewhere, on what came to be know in Britain as 'Black Wednesday', the day the pound sterling was forced to leave the Exchange Rate Mechanism, it was people who spoke anything but standard English who made the events; the Chancellor of the Exchequer was simply left to deliver the decision made by the jockeys of the 'Forex' markets, outside the Treasury building – in standard English of course.

I would like to make three last, essential points on the issue of content. The first is to draw attention to a fundamental shift in our understandings of 'content,' which has taken place over the last two decades or so, and is coming to its culmination now. The second is to give, via an example, a definition of how I see content as needing to be (re)defined. The third is to make a passing reference to older forms of content, and to suggest how and in what ways we may still need that notion.

There is at the moment a deep division on this question of content: and there are several ways to characterise that division. One is to point to the difference between that new form of assessment/validation, the NVQ or the GNVQ, on the one hand, and to GCSE or A level on the other. The latter is based largely on the older conceptions of content, in English at any rate, (even though some very innovative and highly interesting papers are being set by some examination boards). It is complemented by knowing about ways of reading; and ways of writing about one's reading. The NVQ, by total contrast, is *not* focused on knowing *about* something, but on being able to marshal, to deploy one's resources in relation to a particular problem which needs to be dealt with, and to do so in an orderly, organised, predictable (and hence) teachable way. The central pillar of the NVQ assignment is the 'Action Plan'; it sets out a planning, organisational strategy in relation to a problem/task; in terms of assessment it is that which attracts the highest number of marks.

This shift runs deep, much deeper than is recognised – or at least that is my assumption. I have recently begun to think back over the changes in the university system in the Anglo-Saxon world, over the last forty years. The massive expansion of that system in the 1960s and 1970s led to the building of 'new' universities – mostly in the early 1960s. It was a 1950s' scheme which did, however, get a 1960s' inflection, intellectually, academically, and pragmatically, in some places. In Sussex and East Anglia, for instance, 'Schools' were introduced as multidisciplinary groupings which were meant to lead to interdisciplinary ways of working – and sometimes it did. During my time at East Anglia (1971–8) quite fierce arguments were had in the School of English and American Studies (fictionalised later by one of the senior participants in that debate with great popular success as a novel and then a TV series), a grouping of English and American History and Literature, Comparative Literature, Linguistics, and, towards the end of that period, Film, around forms of assessment and their possible justification in terms of graduates' professional and job destinations; and around new interdisciplinary groupings, 'English Studies' for instance (successfully argued for), and 'Cultural Studies' (lost). I remember very clearly the outrage of some 'senior' members of the School at our introduction of the idea of 'relevance'. Relevance was *not* a concept for a Humanities degree in a proper university.

I left East Anglia largely in order to work in a context where relevance was not a term for contemptuous dismissal: in the Australian Colleges of Advanced Education (CAEs) (as, I imagine, in British polytechnics) relevance was at the centre of the enterprise – service to the local community, and to the vocations and professions of that community. But here it became clear to me that this 1970s' move towards relevance demanded precisely the reorganisation of traditional disciplines which the 'Schools' in new universities in England (as in Australia) had introduced. In the CAEs it was essential to assemble people with relevant knowledges around a specific *task*: for instance, 'preparing' people for specific professional paths, or 'delivering' specific knowledge for some external project. But it was the externally defined task which provided the rationale of the new assemblages of people.

The shift had been made from the *production of knowledge*, where relevance could be seen as an illegitimate requirement, to the *assemblage of knowledge for its application in relation to a specific, externally defined demand*, where relevance was the foundational criterion.

In the meantime, of course, the massive inroads of electronic technologies, coupled with the globalisation of production, of finance, and of the media, have come to mean that where there still *is* industry in the 'West', it tends to be tertiary industry – that is, either information industries or service industries. And so the shift I have just described has had a more specific, a narrower articulation, so that now this application of existing knowledge exists in relation, largely, to information in whatever form, and of its management. So the change from the older form of organisation of the (higher) education system can be described as a change from the production of knowledge and of its dissemination, to the assembly of existing knowledge in the service of the management of information.

So while the change looks recent, in relation, say, to the introduction of NVQs and their extension, now, to GNVQs – a spread outward, upward and downward – in my view it is a change which dates back to the mid-1960s at least, and to the purposive change of higher education from an élite to a mass-system. At a time when few, even of the élite, needed to be able to *produce* knowledge, all were nevertheless educated as though they would, and thus imbibed particular attitudes and valuations to knowledge: and these were entirely serviceable for the effective reproduction of that élite. In a mass-higher education system there can simply be no pretence (though my experience at East Anglia in the 1970s illustrates that what has no legitimacy can nevertheless win the day, at least for a while) that all those who pass through it need to be producers of knowledge; given the changed constitution of the economy, all will need to be capable of managing, whatever it may be.

As I have mentioned, this change is spreading rapidly, 'upwards' into higher education, 'side-ways' into schools. GNVQs are simply one surface effect, so that A levels and GCSEs will be affected by this changed notion of content, even where they continue. It affects, in the most profound sense, what we consider to be knowledge, content, skills, etc. For me, the real question, as before, is this: what aspect of this change is 'real', important, essential even, and what is ideology, fashion, chaff, that will be puffed away by the next breeze of fashion.

Clearly, 'management', whether of information or of other 'resources' – human and material – is central in the post-Fordist economies. The idea, however, implied in some of these changes, that we have now done with the production of knowledge is to me perfectly ridiculous, quite as bizarre as the not-so-recently announced End-of-History. So the curriculum will, in my view, need to continue to offer several kinds of contents and 'resources': things to know, things to know about, crucial information about the society's constitution and its history; the analytical and the productive means of producing the new, the innovative, in order to deal with problems not yet imagined or imaginable; as well as the managerial means of deploying existing resources in response to new demands.

First and foremost the curriculum will need to provide *productive understandings*, that is, the means for producing the meanings and forms necessary in a particular instance for the satisfaction of needs and demands of an individual or a group in a particular situation.

Let me use an example which may seem unpropitious: punctuation. Punctuation, if taught at all, is taught in a highly formal fashion, according to rules which are seen simply to be there, with no, or not much, rhyme or reason. However, punctuation is a meaningful system, by which I mean that it is a system used both to make meanings, and to signal what those meanings are. In fact it is an enormously complex and subtle system which is hardly understood. In essence it has the dual function, as I mentioned, of permitting the production of complex structures, consisting of quite diverse elements, and to make these structures readable.

Here is an example. It is a sentence written by an academic who is well published, an accomplished writer; it occurred as part of a text on Mass-Communication Theory:

> *That rejection casts us out to sea on the question of what might that relationship be.*

I will attempt to trace and describe the history of the production of this sentence, paying particular attention to the role and meaning of punctuation in that history.

The sentence has two clauses:

> That rejection casts us out to sea

and

> What might that relationship be?

There is an implied third clause, which I'll list here:

> There is a question (from 'on the question')

These simple clauses correspond to three elements of thinking, three rudimentary ideas, at some stage in the writer's mind. (Of course, I'm not talking here about careful deliberation and execution, but processes that happen at a speed greater than we ourselves can or do usually monitor.) These elements are brought together, using the resources of English syntax, and of punctuation, into the sentence which this writer produced.

One possible form for him to produce might have been:

> That rejection casts us out to sea on the question: what might that relationship be?

Here the second clause is shown as separated, as a discrete element compared to the sentence the author actually did write; this invites

the reader to ponder on that *question* as a distinct element: its separateness as a question is clear.
Another form might have been:

> That rejection casts us out to sea on the question 'What might that relationship be?'

Here the quotation marks show that it is an utterance taken from somewhere else, and quoted here, 'brought into' this writer's text from outside.

Both of these examples use punctuation marks to indicate a quite specific structural relation, and a particular kind of discreteness of the second clause. The sentence written by the author dispenses with quotation marks, even the question mark is regarded as superfluous: the integration of the formerly separate element into the first clause is quite tight. A greater degree of structural work has led to a less overt marking of the structuring.

My own preferred form would have gone one or two steps further, towards even greater integration:

> That rejection casts us out to sea on the question (of) what that relationship might be.

Now we might ask why the writer of the original form stopped the integrating process where he did? What was the meaning he was producing by that? Or, as another question, why do I prefer the more integrated form? (and what does that mean?).

This is a simple example, but it does show punctuation as part of complex and subtle structuring processes – sometimes apparent and visible, sometimes not; and as part of a meaning-making system. It shows punctuation as work, meaning-making work, *of which the writer is in command*. But just to answer my earlier question: why did he not move to the final, more closely integrated form? I can only speculate, but two reasons are clear from my description: *his* form leaves the second clause more clearly as a discrete question, yet moves it a fraction away from the more separate clause of the most speech-like form; it leaves the writing style nearer to the speech-like forms than my more integrated version. To use another idiom: it gives a certain angularity and informality, and perhaps masculinity, to his writing.

So the reasons are both stylistic, and conceptual. But unless we have a view of punctuation as a meaning-full productive resource, these questions cannot even arise. As a small, anecdotal, point I have noticed in my more recent writing, and particularly in this text, a tendency to the (over) use of the 'dash', which I have attempted to tone down in my editing. But to me that points very clearly to a change in my modes of thinking, and in my sense of how I wish to 'speak to' potential readers.

Thinking of punctuation as a meaning-making resource is a new conception of content; but this content has to work on and with something. And here content in that older sense provides the materials to work with: the meanings and values of different cultures; the histories of groups and societies; information about different forms of communication and representation; and information of a theoretical kind, expressed through more or less explicitly or implicitly conveyed information about theories of meaning, reading, writing.

3 People and sociality: identity, personality, subjectivity

Reading and writing

The decisive distinctions between reading and writing are not cognitive or semiotic but social and cultural ones; they do, however, have cognitive and psychological effects and through these further social and cultural effects. The distinctions have to do with the social and cultural status of written text; with differential access to producing texts and to reading texts. These are themselves effects of social and economic histories, and of present social configurations. The learning of writing is hugely influenced by the kind of access to the forms of language which is most characteristic in the social group in which a child grows up: this access provides an initial and often ultimately decisive structuring of the child's path into writing.

Semiotically speaking, there is a continuity between reading and writing: writing is the production of new signs from existing and available resources, and so is reading. Reading is the *internal* production of what the semiotician Charles Sanders Peirce called an 'interpretant', which constitutes the *internal* production of the new sign for the reader (or viewer, or sensor) from the externally available sign, the sign that is read. Writing is the *external* production of signs, for a readership usually consisting of more than one reader.

Reading is the means whereby new cultural, social, semiotic materials become available to me. Whether I have access to certain semiotic materials, and what kind of materials these are, affects what kind of cognitive/transformative processes I will engage in, and around what kinds of structures and materials these transformative processes occur. Cognitively, there is a crucial difference between the possibilities of producing signs in reading only, and the production of external signs in writing (or drawing, making of any kind). The latter has the social consequences of making me a participant in my group's constant new production of its representational resources; it also has the cognitive and subjective consequence of making me the producer of my own resources of representation in what remains still society's most valued mode, writing. This is no more nor less than the entirely common experience had by any writer that 'writing it down' makes this 'it' newly and productively useable in ways in which it was not, prior to 'its' being written down. Externalisation and objectification are central processes in cognitive development.

In the (social semiotic) theory of writing which I put forward here, reading is the process whereby new materials can be 'assimilated', can be transformed, and become transformative in terms of an individual's existent set of resources, and thereby of her or his subjectivity.

Theories of reading, and practices of reading deriving from these, are crucial both in the formation of identity and subjectivity and in the possibilities of new production of signs. If texts are multimodal, reading is a complex activity in which the reader attends to the different modes in which signs are produced, and has to integrate complexes of signs from the different modes into a single, coherent reading. As an exercise, try to list the modes of representation which are involved in a film, and imagine the work done by the viewer in drawing a coherent reading from that complex text. Different practices of reading entail different dispositions, identities, subjectivities. Theories which lay stress on a single mode; which stress closely defined units with impermeable boundaries; which hold to a decoding view rather than one of transformation; will envisage and encourage a specific kind of subjectivity. A theory which stresses the multimodality of texts; the reader's power in setting the boundaries of the unit to be read; and which sees reading as a process of transformation; will envisage and encourage a different subjectivity.

Evidence for the processes and effects of reading is always indirect. Direct observation is impossible; and although observing readers reading can provide material for speculation, it remains just that. The evidence which I have begun to focus on is somewhat different and it is available to any teacher in every classroom. It consists of signs produced by a reader following their reading of some material, usually immediately, but not necessarily so. Take, for instance, the example opposite.

Figure 6: *'Look, 'I've done it!'*

The (four-year-old) child had asked her parent to write 'thank you', in order to write it herself on a card for a friend. When she produced the sign in Figure 6 she showed it to her parent excitedly, 'Look, I've done it!' The sign shows that a fundamental principle employed in reading as much as in writing is what I call the *motivated sign*, that is, the assumption that in our making of meaningful signs, whether in reading or writing, we look for and assume an integral relation between form and meaning – the one expressive of the other. Here the child's implicit motivation for joining form and meaning might be 'linked elements go together'; this will later be generalised by this child to the broader notion of 'coherence'. It enables her to read the initial two elements in the parent's carelessly written THANK YOU as a single unit. The child's *interest* in finding a meaningful connection between form and meaning provides the motivation for the production of the (assumed/inferred) internal sign: wishing to be able to write 'thank you' leads her to seek the principles of the constitution of units in the parent's (unhelpful) model.

The crucial issue is to see both reading and writing as entirely active processes, never merely as the relatively passive, mechanistic process of 'decoding' of a stable text by a reader, a process which adds information to the reader; and similarly not to see writing as a mechanical process of reproduction. The latter is, of course, entirely antithetical to traditions of English teaching; and exhortations which are currently made in this regard by right-wing ideologues have formed no part of the English teaching tradition.

However, what I wish to put forward differs, I believe, from that tradition. It has stressed the expressive power of language, and of narrative. That presupposes a relatively stable relation between a medium of expression – say, language – and a system of meanings, whether seen as personal and individual or as social and cultural. Creativity, in this view, arises from novel uses of existing resources. It leaves the system intact. In my view reading is a *transformative process*: the child; reading the TH of 'thank you' shows that she approached this sign, in the external world, with sets of interpretative principles, through which she apprehended that bit of the external world which was at that time, through her interest, in her focus. Writing, in much the same way, is a transformative process, whereby a *new* sign is produced by a writer, in response to a whole complex of factors. Writing is never merely reproductive; it is always more than expressive; it is an act of transformation, in which the writer transforms the expressive/representational means; transforms her or his own subjectivity; and therefore transforms the world in which the newly made sign appears. Writing, as the making of signs in any medium, *changes the system*; it is not the same system after the writer's writing.

As a metaphor for this view of sign-making take the image in Figure 7 (opposite): made by an eight-year old Nigerian child, who had, at that time, been in England for a year. The drawing was made in response to the teacher's reading of Snow White, and his subsequent request to the class to write the story, and to draw a picture. Clearly the child had made his own sense of the story; a result of his cultural/cognitive resources; and from that new sign he produced in his drawing an entirely novel image, the queen of the story of Snow White as she has never been seen before.

This stands for me as the innovative potential of the making of new meaning out of the resources of pluriculturalism.

Figure 7

Some thoughts on the politics of the literacy debate

Literacy, I imagine we all agree, is an essential ingredient for participation by a citizen in the public, social, cultural, economic and political life of their society. It is therefore not in the least bit surprising that the issue of literacy has become such a crucial site of debate and contestation, of political struggle. This is sharpened by the point I have made several times: that we find ourselves in times of far-reaching social and economic change, with little certainty about the shape of tomorrow. The struggle is thus not simply one over competing but settled versions of what this citizen should be; it is given a sharpness by the very fact that – despite my rhetorical certitude – we are, all of us, in the dark about the shape of the future.

For me, then, the politics of the literacy debate has to be seen in this light. What contents of the new kind do we want children now in our schools to know; who do we want them to be; what values should they treat as natural, normal, as human, in order to live full lives in the changed world of tomorrow? The parameters of debates around literacy are, as for much of the English curriculum, far too often set narrowly in the present. Our conception of literacy should shift these parameters, and point to the possibilities of a different horizon.

Literacy, like no other element in the culture of our society, is bound up with cultural and social possibilities. It represents a society's means of representing the world to itself; it is its means of representing itself to itself. In the possibilities of understanding the meanings of a society and having a part in making meanings for themselves and for their society, individuals find their means of becoming social persons. Literacy, as a culture's possibility of making its images of itself and of its world, is foundational in the shaping of the future. The means of (making) representations which we provide for children and for adults, are the means which enable them to be fully human and fully social.

It is here where curriculum issues begin to arise. If we agree on the desirable and even essential characteristics of the citizen of tomorrow (most of industry and commerce regards these as essential *now*), we have to ask whether the contents and implied pedagogies of our literacy curricula foster such characteristics, or are indifferent to them, or are positively antagonistic to them. The habits of representation which we naturalise in the literacy curricula and in the pedagogic practices associated with them, whether in reading or in writing, have their inevitable effects in what children take as usual, as natural, as given; and set the boundaries on the possibilities of the making of the self by each individual child.

It is essential to examine a curriculum and its methods of teaching from that point of view. If we represent literacy, in the curriculum, as a matter of fixed, immutable rules, we encourage a different attitude to the one suggested by a representation of literacy as a set of resources shaped by society and constantly reshaped by each individual reader and writer. The former encourages acceptance of *what is*; a certain attitude to authority; a limitation accepted and internalised by the individual. The latter encourages curiosity about how things have come to be as they are; a certain attitude to individual responsibility and agency; and an internalisation of the individual as active, creative, and expansive.

At the moment the literacy debate is polarised in public debate, broadly speaking, between two positions, seen as entirely incompatible. I say 'in public' to make an absolutely essential distinction between what happens everyday in nearly every classroom in schools and what happens nearly everyday in every newspaper in the country – fuelled by the too often politically strategic production of reports of research carried out by one group or another.

In the midst of this, teachers remain admirably pragmatic, basing their practice on their own experience, on that of their colleagues, and on a judicious use of research produced and filtered to them in different ways – through the media, through inservice, through their professional journals and organisations.

To characterise these poles, I'll use two abbreviations: one I shall call 'the coding view'; the other I shall call 'the contextual view'. The 'coding view' is represented by highly formalistic views of literacy: literacy as a formal code, for instance a formal code which connects the sounds of speech in a describable fashion to the graphic elements of writing. Competence in literacy is seen to lie in the mastery of this connecting code. As long as you can transliterate from either the sounds of speech to the graphic elements of writing, or vice-versa, you are literate, in this view. The 'contextual view' is represented by entirely anti-formal 'environmental' views of literacy: literacy is a matter of using any one of a whole range of cues available in the environment, not just of the text but of the reader, to (re)construct the meaning of a text. Competence in literacy is seen to lie in the accomplishment of the task of drawing on any one of these to make sense of a text. As long as you can make some meaning from a text, you are literate. The text is – to put it into an overly exaggerated form – merely a prompt to semiotic activity.

Now the fact that these are (close to being) caricature versions of the opposing positions does not mean that they do not exist in pretty well pure form. There is no need to attach labels such as 'phonics', or 'whole language/real books' to these positions, though one could. The point is that they exist *in public debates*, in the media for instance; they are unlikely to correspond to the views of every practitioner. But in their public, politically inspired form, they guide *the direction of the practice*. If today some media organ on the right has a front-page story on illiteracy, as there was, for instance, on the day I first wrote this, then this will have not only a political effect, but practical pedagogic effects.

Predictably enough, I think both contain essential elements of truth and both have disabling weaknesses. Both point to politics in a much broader sense. The 'coding view' focuses on providing access to what we can call 'the text-to-be-read'. In this approach no problems arise about precisely what the text is – that is, the text is taken, unproblematically, to be the material thing which is immediately here, in front of me, to be read, whether a word, a sentence, or a larger unit. It has clear and clearly recognisable boundaries. No questions arise about the necessary larger knowledge which any reader must always bring to the reading of any text for reading to become possible. So, for instance, words are seen as essentially, or even exclusively, phonological–graphological units: their meaning is not an issue. In the reading of a whole text no acknowledgement is made, or can be made, of the essential process of connecting this text here with the many other texts which I need to invoke, however unconsciously, in my mind when I am reading any text. Connections, it could be said, are ruled out.

This approach implicitly suggests a particular pedagogy: precisely one that rules out connection; that takes units as given; that treats tasks as routines to be learned rather than as processes to be performed. The politics of such a curriculum and its pedagogies are clear enough: certainly, the child inducted into reading within this approach is unlikely to take from it notions of individually motivated action or of innovative solution. Rather, there are messages of a strong orientation towards an acceptance of existing states of affairs, and systems of rules. As an education for a future society or economy – a workplace dependent on ingrained habits of flexibility, change, and innovation – it raises serious questions.

The 'contextual view' focuses on the limitless world of meaning, to which the text in front of the reader is simply a prompt. In a sense, in this view the formal properties of the concrete text in front of the reader give access to the real text-to-be-read, which is taken as being the world potentially. The real focus is the reader's capacity as a maker of meaning. In a quite strong sense, the material text here is seen as no more than the provision of a series of prompts for explorations: the question of what the text-to-be-read is, is here as unproblematic as it is in the other case, though in the opposite sense. Reading is seen as the creative process of meaning-making: the concrete text in front of the reader is merely a starting point. If formalism – being tied too excessively to narrow notions of form – is the problem in the first approach, then formalism is an equal problem here, by its negation. In effect, the formal composition of a text is not treated as a serious question – form is not seen as having any real meaning. In the reading process envisaged in the contextual view, the actual limits set by the text-to-be-read are seen as limitations to be overcome rather than as constraints to be recognised and included as an essential aspect of reading. Literalness, it could be said, is ruled out.

Let me introduce the briefest, perhaps metaphoric, example of what I have in mind when I talk about the 'limits set by the text-to-be-read'. The example concerns the effect of forms of writing systems – alphabetic vs logographic (or ideographic) – on a child's engagement with writing. The two images overleaf show that engagement by two girls, both about three and a half years of age, with the formal characteristics of the scripts in their environment. Let me say, somewhat contentiously, that both are at this stage 'drawing' the scripts, rather than writing them.

The children, in engaging with 'writing', have to uncover for themselves the deep logic of each script. In the case of the girl learning alphabetic writing (see Figure 8), four bits of that logic are apparent here as far as she is concerned: linearity; sequentiality; and connectedness; of relatively simple, repeated and repeatable shapes. This is, however implicitly it is learned, one of the most fundamental aspects of writing which she seems to have deduced from the model here. I do not wish to maintain, even for a moment, that this is *the* settled truth for her; rather her engagement with writing is a constant, incessant, relentless analytic enterprise – as I will show in a moment, and the truth about it will not be settled for many years. But it is one early, fundamental truth, and it is established by her, for herself, early on.

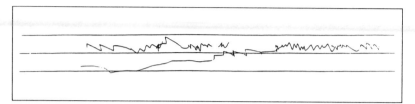

Figure 8: *Alphabetic script*

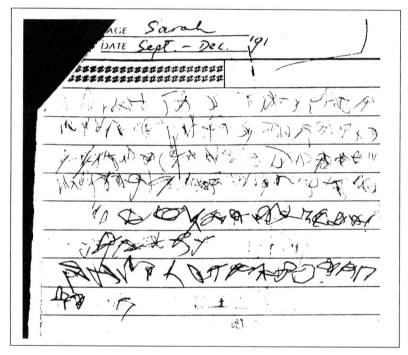

Figure 9: *Drawing logographic script*

In the case of the girl learning logographic (or ideographic) writing (see Figure 9), another kind of logic – again as far as she is concerned – is learned here: linearity yes; but of discrete elements, which are not connected; each of which is highly complex in itself and is clearly bounded; not repeated or highly repeatable. As a logic about the deep meaning of written language it is fundamentally different, and must have – though I am merely speculating here – the most far-reaching effects on notions of what language is, and what writing does. Out of this learning both girls will make, for themselves, particular kinds of rationality: in both cases rationalities so deeply embedded that they will not be available for the writer's own inspection, and rationalisations which are deeply different for the learner of the alphabetic and the logographic forms of representation.

There is another foundational difference here, which plays quite differently into a child's move into writing. Alphabetic writing is, in as far as it is connected with spoken language, a transliteration of the *sounds* of language into discrete graphic elements, letters, representing those sounds. It is only at a second step an association of ideas with these letters. Logographic or ideographic writing on the other hand represents not sounds but *ideas* in the form of (highly abstracted and conventionalised) images. It is only at a second step that there is an association of sounds to these ideas.

It might be thought, reasonably, that the girl drawing the alphabetic script is perhaps not as 'advanced' as the girl drawing the logographic script. So let me introduce a drawing she made of a balsa-wood model of a Tyrannosaurus Rex, standing in her room.

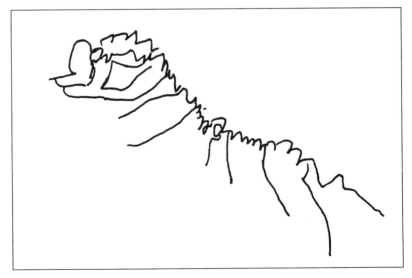

Figure 10: *Tyrannosaurus Rex*

'Competence' seems, to me, not to be the issue. There is another, a deeper issue here, though. In a sense, Chinese writing invites the child to continue on the same path as the 'writing' (to be contentious again) of the Tyrannosaurus Rex, and it makes *that* the path into writing; whereas alphabetic writing systems interpose the analysis of sound as a first step into reading and writing. My assumption is that the former, putting the representation of thoughts and ideas in the form of pictures first, must accord with the child's own meaning-making disposition much more closely than the alphabetic system does.

The contextual view suggests a particular pedagogy (which has been described at length by its opponents): concessive, permissive, liberal. Texts are not to be treated as authoritative; limits are to be transcended; formalism, as attention to form, is seen as a limitation on human freedom. The implied politics are just as clear as in the first case. The child inducted into this approach is unlikely to take from it notions of a need for close engagement with the agendas of others, towards the need for recognition of and action within limits, the acceptance of rules, the existence of states of affairs. While this approach seems to hold out the promise of an education of an individual suited for a society in which change is a given and innovation a necessity, I have serious reservations about this approach. In a world seen as having no rules and no boundaries, the possibilities for creativity and innovation disappear. Where nothing is given nothing can be a surprise. Where nothing is old, nothing can be new. In a deep sense it is an approach which works against innovation.

The 'coding view' as much as the 'contextual view' both regard form as vacuous. For the former, form is central and vacuous; for the latter, form is marginal and vacuous. Both produce pedagogies and politics which are, in my view, deeply inadequate; neither is truly enabling for the child as future citizen.

As my script example might demonstrate, both approaches must be puzzling to a child-learner. In phonics (to take it as an example) the relation between the text-to-be-read (whether as the smallest unit, the letter or letter sequence, or the word, or the larger texts) and meaning is portrayed as arbitrary, and sustained only by an authoritatively imposed rule-system. As a view of how meaning is made and encoded this is deeply antithetical to the child's own experience. In the whole-language/real books approach the relation between the text-to-be-read and its meaning is equally portrayed as arbitrary, sustained in this case not by an authoritatively imposed system of rules maintaining arbitrary connections, but produced in an essentially unconstrained fashion by the reader in the process of reading. While there may seem to be stronger affinities between this approach and the child's own, implicitly held view, the grounds for deciding on a particular reading are always unavailable, as are the grounds, therefore, for arriving at an consensus about a reading or even the grounds for establishing the grounds of disagreement.

In the child's own view purpose and form are tightly linked; the seeming affinity with the contextual view is spurious and rests on a disabling misconception of the child, and of childish action, as anarchic, unfocused, 'doing whatever comes into their heads'. Children, however, are totally precise in what they do. Let me give an illustration of this issue, of what is to be read, and how. Take any comic. With a 'coding view' the text-to-be-read, presumably, is the verbal text; leaving aside the question of how child readers know the order in which the textual segments are to be read; or what effect is to be attributed to the images. As an example, here is the verbal text of the first page of a *Dennis the Menace* comic:

> *'Going to help me lay these slabs for our patio?' [Walter Daddykins];*
> *'We love being helpful' [Slablaying for beginners]; 'NNN! All together chummies – LIFT!' 'HO-HO!'; 'HMM! Don't think you're quite up to this' [Slablaying for Beginners]; 'we'll help'; 'Gasp! Not like the Menaces to be helpful!'; 'This one goes here...now, a dark one there...'; [Soon]; 'Squeal! How frightening!'; 'Tremble! words like 'YA' Scare us!' 'Gnashee!'; 'Naughty boys! put them in a proper design!'. [More on back page]*

The verbal text by itself is clearly not sufficient to give a reader meaning; it depends precisely on the co-presence of the visual images, which in this as in most instances are tightly *complementary* to the verbal text. That is, the visual text is not, as the commonsense notions of illustration tends to have it, merely an illustration of what is already said verbally; rather it is a complement to the verbal text. Or, to make this point more strongly and equally validly, the verbal text is a complement to the visual text; it provides *completion* to the visual text. The point about the 'tight complementarity' is easily made: pronouns (and other pro-forms) such as 'this' or 'here' ('this one goes here') get their meaning precisely from the complementary visual text. All of this text is constructed in this fashion.

To draw a general point from this, one might say that the reading of any textual element always draws on and depends on a simultaneous consideration of the co-text of the text (or textual element) being read – whether that co-text is other verbal text, or text in another medium of communication.

A point emerges here, equally, about the real books/whole language approach: at times, in that approach, the visual part of the text is seen as a means of providing essential cues for the reading of the verbal text, which is, again, the 'illustration' view – where the visual text 'stands for' the real world so to speak, in which we can find the contextual cues that give us access to the full meaning of a verbal text. But again, if you look at any comic you will see that the visual text does not cast clear light on the meanings of the verbal items: it makes its own, complementary – and not parallel – meanings.

The teaching and learning of reading, perhaps even more than the teaching of writing, is such an important and highly valued practice in our societies, that it has the most far-reaching consequences. What we think reading is, and the practices and habits we therefore constantly foster and encourage in the teaching of reading, have far-reaching consequences for those who learn to read. The teaching of reading contributes strongly to a student's dispositions not only towards verbal texts, but towards the whole world of meaning: on the one hand anxiously confined and limited to an accepted system of rules, which is seen as relating forms and meanings in an arbitrary fashion; on the other hand set adrift in a world seemingly without rules or stability of meaning. My own, perhaps paradoxical solution, lies in an essential combination of what I regard as elements of truth about each position: form is meaning *always*, in all instances, at every level, so that an absolute attention must be paid to details of form; and form always exists in co-texts, of whatever kinds, which must always be read simultaneously, for their separate expression of meaning.

Out of all of these, read together, comes the meaning of a text. In cultures where language is treated as the central and most highly valued medium of communication, the 'non-verbal' elements seem to supplement the verbal text. We are entering an age in which the visual may (already) be central. Perhaps then we will speak of the non-visual text, or perhaps the non-gestural text, to refer to language.

Meaning is produced in a constant and complex interplay between the meanings of the form read at this instant, and the meanings of the forms in the surrounding co-text, which includes, crucially, the meanings held by the reader who is herself a repository of meaning.

To move to a slightly different level, I find the concept of *habitus* as it has been developed most recently by the French sociologist Pierre Bourdieu most useful in thinking about this issue. In his introduction to a collection of writings *Language and Symbolic Power*, the editor of that collection, John Thompson, provides the following description of the term *habitus*:

> the habitus is a set of dispositions which incline agents to act and react in certain ways. The dispositions generate practices, perceptions and attitudes which are 'regular' without being consciously co-ordinated or governed by any 'rule'. The dispositions which constitute the habitus are inculcated, structured, durable, generative and transposable . . . [they] are acquired through a gradual process of inculcation in which early childhood experiences are particularly important. Through a myriad of mundane processes of training and learning, such as those involved in the inculcation of table manners ('sit up straight', 'don't talk with your mouth full', etc.) the individual acquires a set of dispositions which literally mould the body and become second nature. The dispositions produced thereby are also structured in the sense that they unavoidably reflect the social conditions within which they were acquired. An individual from a working-class background for instance, will have acquired dispositions which are different in certain respects from those acquired by individuals who were brought up in a middle-class milieu . . . Structured dispositions are also durable . . . they endure through the life history of the individual . . . [they] are generative and transposable in the sense that they are capable of generating a multiplicity of practices and perceptions in fields other that those in which they were originally acquired.
> (in Bourdieu, 1990, pages 12–13)

The deeper implication of moving to a consideration of reading in terms such as these is that it forces us to think of reading not simply in the pragmatic terms of supplying a crucial skill, but sees reading instead in terms of its effect on (changing) the 'personality', the subjectivity of a reader. In education the basic issue, always, is the concern with the characteristics of the human being who is being educated: what kind of individual, what kind of social being do we imagine as the result of our teaching, and as the result of their learning in the context of our teaching. This is the point of this book: the point about imagined citizens and imagined futures.

My perspective on literacy seems all the more necessary given the fundamental factors of multiculturalism, and of technological change. The former is producing deep-reaching social changes, which are not fully assessable at the moment; the latter is unmaking the contours of a hitherto settled world in different ways. Both have the most profound effects on literacy, and therefore on reading.

Multiculturalism brings into one society the very different modes of representation (with their different valuation) of different ethnic/linguistic/cultural groups. It brings into sharp focus the fact that the means of representation, and the practices of representation which a culture has developed, have profound effects on the constitution of personality, of habitus, of subjectivity. Multiculturalism forces us to consider what we might otherwise have continued to ignore. Representational resources are culture-bound, culture-specific, are themselves the product of histories of cultural practices in all cultural and social domains, and shape those who use them in very different ways.

My example of the two girls' responses to writing systems may stand as a metaphor for this point, which reaches into every area of meaning-making. Think of front pages of contemporary European newspapers: one *The Sun* in England, the other the *Frankfurter Allgemeine* in Germany, the latter still *all* print, no images, no colour. My contention is that each makes available a different set of representational resources, and habituates its readers to very different kinds of reading. Over time, insistently, the habituated readers of *The Sun* and of the *Frankfurter Allgemeine* become different readers. I won't go into great detail here, but one or two indications of my thinking will allow you to follow and develop (or reject!) my line of argument. The reader of the *Frankfurter Allgemeine*, has become habituated to seeing written language as the major representational resource – the reader of *The Sun* is becoming habituated to seeing the visual in the form of images (and colour) as the major representational resource. The reader of the *Frankfurter Allgemeine* is becoming habituated to reading with concentration (as indicated by the length of the articles, by the density of the spacing; by the typeface used, by the sentence-syntax); the reader of *The Sun* has become habituated to an immediacy of apprehension, a disinclination to concentrated reading perhaps (as indicated by the screamer headlines; the very large image; the brevity of the written articles; the very small amount of written language; etc.). The reader of the *Frankfurter Allgemeine* is presented on the front page with about a dozen articles, so that the world is shown as complex and varied; the reader of *The Sun* is usually presented with one article, so the world is shown as a place that can be made sense of in simple terms.

One response to my argument here is to say that the difference lies not in a difference of culture, but in a difference of class. However, a look at the front page of the German *Bild Zeitung*, the equivalent broadly, in terms of readership, shows a total difference with the clarity of look of *The Sun*; it is an intensification of the multiplicity of the *Frankfurter Allgemeine* into the direction of anarchy, using images and colour of course. It is possible to say that the *Frankfurter Allgemeine* and *Bild Zeitung* share more features than the (broadly equivalent) *Frankfurter Allgemeine* and *Daily Telegraph*; or, that *The Guardian* has more in common with *The Sun* (from this point of view) than *The Guardian* has with the *Frankfurter Allgemeine* or other German papers of a similar readership.

Of course, cross-national cultural differences are matched by intranational cultural differences, say, in the classrooms of multicultural Britain. The forms of literacy have significant effects on the kinds of writers and readers, and on the kinds of social beings who are the habituated users of these forms. In the construction of literacy curricula we need to be fully aware of the meanings of form, for any number of reasons, just as we have to be aware of the formal differences between spoken and written language. The differences have effects in culture, but also in cognition, in ways of knowing, and in possibilities of forming knowledge.

The further point, at least as crucial for me, is the recognition that if formal difference points to cultural and cognitive difference, then these differences represent a potential cultural reservoir of enormous significance, always providing that they can be brought into productive use. A student, formed in the experience of formal difference as deeply valuable cultural difference, has at her or his disposition the possibility of responding to specific problems with the resources not just of one culture and its literacy, but of the knowledge that other solutions are available in the representational resources of other cultures. It is steps like this which will move us towards the production of a naturalised, deep-seated culture of innovation.

Representational resources and subjectivity

The reigning view of language during this century has been provided by a particular reading of Saussure's *Course in General Linguistics* (1974, first published 1915). That is a view of language as a system which is beyond the effect of the individual language user; she or he *makes use* of the system *(langue)* but they do not in the use of this system *(parole)* produce any changes in the system. Although Saussure himself was intensely interested in history, those who produced the dominant interpretation of his ideas for this century focused on the a-historical, a-social, anti-individual aspects of Saussure's theory. That has led to, and has legitimated a century of mainstream work in linguistics in which language was severed from history and society, and from the effective action of individual language users. Of course, other important work in language theory took place during this period, for example the work of the Danish linguist Louis Hjelmslev, of Prague School linguistics, of Firth and Halliday, of American anthropological and ethnographic work on language – the work of scholars such as Sapir and Hymes. But it will serve as a useable sketch of the largely American mainstream in linguistics.

It is this hegemonic view which has severed language from history and society, from the effect of individual action, which has led to a turning-away, rightly in my view, of most English teachers, from linguistics, which they saw as formal and sterile. This same view has underpinned the notion of 'language *acquisition*'. This is based on a psycholinguistic model of language (produced largely in the Chomskyan school of linguistics which assumes the existence of an innate predisposition in human beings to language, more or less developed and articulated; for instance in the influential notion of the 'Language Acquisition Device'). In this model the task of the language learner is to *acquire* their language on the basis of these innate structures.

One constant effect of these approaches is precisely that implied in the acquisition-metaphor, a metaphor which treats the role of the acquirer as a relatively mechanical, inert one: simply that of acquisition. There are more far-reaching, profound implications of this model, including its implicit notions of a-social individuality, of particular forms of sociality, and from the point of view of my discussion, of who we are as humans.

There is an important, but partial, truth in this mainstream view: we must understand the human brain, and its effect on all human action, language included. As a picture of the whole truth about language it is a depressingly distorted view, and its filtering into educational theory and practice has been baleful. It is essential, therefore, in any project of rethinking English to have a plausible theory of language. I put forward an alternative view. It sees language as a predominantly socially, culturally, and historically produced system. This is not to deny the existence of physiological/neural organisations of the brain which have profound consequences for the possibilities of human language, as indeed for all human systems of representation. I do not engage in a debate here because the issue is too significant to deal with superficially. In my alternative view, individual users of language – or of any other human system of representation – are, at the same time as being the users, of that system, the *(re)makers* of their systems of representation, out of their social and cultural histories and present positions, and out of their affective dispositions, their *interests* at the point of making signs. Individual interest, itself an expression in complex ways of the interests of social groups, is constantly at work in the making of each individual sign, and in the shaping of the individual's system of representation. Consequently, the systems of representation used by any one individual are *both the product of their own actions* in the social and cultural locations of their histories, and *the effect of the socially and culturally available resources*. Conversely, the systems of representation of any social and cultural group are the effects of the collective actions of individual makers of signs. Social and individual communicative, and representational activities are linked in a complex but tightly integrated mesh.

The individual's work/action in the making of new signs out of existing representational resources is cognitive work. It is transformative work involving the available representational resources in the context of a constant 'reading' of the relevant aspects of the semiotic environment. When a three-year-old child, labouring to climb a steep slope, says 'This is a heavy hill' he uses an available resource. This is a minimal position: my assumption is that what is altered in the remaking of the means of representation is not just the potential of cognitive action but the cognitive state or disposition of the individual. That is, what is changed is the individual's *subjectivity*. The child who can draw a circle, who has produced therefore the representational resource of 'circles' is, in a real conceptual/cognitive sense, not the same as the individual who previously had available to him 'circular scribbles'. His potential for producing meaning has increased and altered. With that a change has occurred in who he *is* and who he *can be*; a change produced by the child for himself. Changed subjectivities entail changed potentials for identity, where I use the word 'identity' to indicate the production of a relatively stable external display, a 'persona', from a particular configuration of internal resources or states; out of a given subjectivity.

Representational resources, produced by an individual, are thus directly related to, and are an alternative aspect of, subjectivity. To put it simply: as you make more and more of your culture's language for yourself, not only do you become more adept at communicating, you become a different person. So a formal description of the semiotic repertoire of an individual can be seen as a description of the characteristics of subjectivity. 'Development' has to be seen in intimate connection with the possibilities of representation.

In this context it becomes important to understand the representational and cognitive potentials of the different semiotic modes – language, gesture, images, other kinds of making – used by and available to any individual. In the context of schooling it becomes essential to understand the assembly of representational modes used by children, and their potentials of interaction. It has usually been assumed in mainstream educational theories that cognition rests on language; or, if different representational modes have been considered (painting, drawing, dancing, music, 'play', etc.), it has been assumed that each remains a discrete area of cognition and of individual action. In non-mainstream theories and practices – the work, for instance, of Steiner, Montessori, as of others – an integrated approach has formed the basis of the foundation of schooling through teaching and learning. It may be that now, more than in previous times, there is a strong distinction between the semiotic modes available and valued in school – language largely, though the modes of mathematics and science are highly significant – and those available and valued outside school, where the visual, sound other than as language, and the body as expressive and communicational medium are highly significant. Children move constantly in and between both, and it is their (often unrecognised) task to construct mediations between both.

Different semiotic modes have different possibilities for representation, and have differential values and placing in a culture as means of public communication. These are both inherent, and culturally produced. Inherent in the visual modes are the enormously greater modal resources of colour, of shading, of signalling of degrees of the sign-maker's 'involvement' in the represented event (via angles of view), and of relations of power signalled through the horizontal and vertical angles of represented object to viewer (literally 'looking up to', 'looking down on', 'looking askance at'). Culturally produced, for instance, in that forms of communication which are not publicly acknowledged, recognised, or valued, tend to be less developed, less articulated, than those which are. An obvious example is that of the semiotic mode of 'gesture'. Not only do cultural groups differ significantly in the use, development, articulation and valuation of gesture, but where gesture becomes the primary means of communication, as in sign-languages (e.g. American Sign Language, British Sign Language), this mode becomes richly developed and articulated.

This may make it clearer how 'mode of representation' and 'subjectivity' are mutually interacting and interdependent. The possibilities and limitations, the degree of development and articulation of each medium, make possible the individual's differential production of subjectivity. All members of any society have available to them a range of modes of representation and of communication, and subjectivities are the products of their use of complexes of representational and communicational modes, and of their interaction, suffused by the modalities of effect. Despite the school system's emphasis on language and on writing in particular, some children grow up to be cartoonists, dancers, carpenters, mechanics, physicists, painters, musicians, architects, designers, mathematicians, etc.; that is, *they* insist on using other modes of representation as their favoured modes of expression, representation and communication.

Clearly, the school's valuation of modes of representation and of communication, in itself a product of the valuation of the representational and communicational modes of particular cultural groups and societies, is of great significance here. It engages, it meshes differentially with the value systems which different children bring to school. If a school values language in written form most highly, it may be less sensitive to the forms of language which children bring with them from backgrounds more oriented to the spoken form. The problems of a child's engagement with and future path into the valued representational forms of schooling can be traced to these early periods, to their assessment by the child, and their effect on the child. The speech–writing difference – on a larger level the distinction of oral vs literate cultures – is one major issue even in so-called literate societies, and it is slowly being recognised and theorised. The differential uses and valuations of other modes of communication and representation is less recognised: at least not in formal, public accounts, rather than in the practical understandings of teachers – but it is an equally significant issue.

In multicultural societies, as all western technologically developed societies now are, this problem is vastly increased, though not necessarily better recognised or acknowledged. The formation of cohesive, if not unified societies rests, among other economic and political matters, on a full recognition of this factor: and schooling has a central part in this.

In a view of English as central in the making of a culture of innovation the production of subjectivity is in the centre, between social and cultural possibilities and forces on the one hand – available resources, structures of power – and the individual's action in the making of signs on the other. An issue such as gender-specific forms of communication can find an explanation here, resolving the oppositional or paradoxical positions of 'imposition' ('gender positions are imposed on us'), and 'internalisation' ('we internalise the models which are available around us', for instance). Out of the available resources, in the structure of cultural and social forces, *the child* produces signs which are produced out of, reflect and encode *her* interest. That interest includes her 'reading' of the semiotic environment; her criteria of relevance – which is where family structures, for instance, become so significant; and it includes her interest in possibilities of communication. Her interest in the making of signs may range from dispositions called 'conformity' to those called 'resistance'; be subversive or solidary. Whether in solidarity or in subversion, the child's own production of her representational resources is intimately connected, in a relation of reciprocity, with *her* production of her subjectivity. This is as true of the learning of writing as it is of the learning of other representational modes. In the following two extracts (from economics essays written by two students in their final year of high school in the New South Wales education system) my account of the learning of writing may provide some suggestions of the ongoing development of previously produced and learned gendered subjectivities, put forward here as one possible means of understanding these issues.

It is normally assumed that more technically oriented school-subjects suit boys better than girls (where 'suit' is a complex and euphemistic term for the histories of gender-arrangements in relation to school subjects). On the face of it, Economics, with its technicities might suit boys more than girls. Yet the writer of the extract (from essay) B, a young woman, writes a text which is more 'fluent', more 'polished', than that of the writer of the extract (from essay) A. Her essay was given a grade of 18 out of 20; that of A a grade of 12 out of 20. The economics 'content' of each, the competence in the subject matter was judged to be about the same by several economics teachers to whom I showed the two essays.

Extract A

Question 22: Need for tax reform in Australia

The main pattern of the Australian tax system is a heavy reliance on income tax, it has a tendency to cause inflation. It also has relied on partly the keynesian policies, the equity of the system has left something to be desired causing uneven income distribution and other problems. Recent suggestions for improving the system, which were outlined in the Sydney Morning Herald in 'Tax and You' are a capital gains tax, Broad Based Indirect tax system, Retail tax, wealth tax and Gift and Death duties. All of the above taxes have major problems in trying to implement them.

The heavy reliance on personal income tax is because of the decreasing reliance on other taxes and it is a big revenue collector. From 1948 to 1983/84 it has increased approximately 9.2%, i.e. from 42%–51.2%. A decrease in company tax from 15.4% in 1948 to 10% in 1983/4 is because the government has tried to get the companies to increase production, eventually leading to an expanding economy.

The reason why this system causes inflation is because they tried to adopt old methods for different and new problems, i.e. Keynsian policies which were to get the government to increase revenue to companies in form of investment which needs increased production leads.

Extract B

Question 22: Need for taxation reform in Australia Year 12

The recent call for taxation reform in Australia has been prompted by the fact that Australia's taxation system is becoming less equitable. Therefore, the major consideration for tax reform in Australia is the equity of the new system.

At present, Australia's tax system relies fairly heavily on the tax receipts from PAYE taxpayers. The past 35 years has seen an increasingly heavy burden bourn by income taxpayers. Their share of the total taxation revenue has increased from 42% in 1948/49 to 51.2% in 1983/84. This has been combined with a fall in taxation revenue from Company tax and customs duty. This heavy burden bourne by personal income taxpayers in Australia has been one of the major reasons for the call for tax reform. So, at present, we have a tax system that relies heavily on income tax.

The equity of Australia's tax system has also been questioned. Twenty years ago you had to earn 17.6 times the average weekly earnings (AWE) before you fell into the then top tax bracket of 66c in the dollar.

Today this figure has fallen to approximately 2 times the AWE. This has meant that people in the middle income groups have fallen into the top tax bracket. So, in the past a pay rise for all Australian workers left the poor generally better off, didn't affect the rich much, but the middle income groups 'got it in the neck'. Their incomes (by no means gigantic) pushed them into the top bracket.

Without going into great descriptive detail here let me say the following. The relative (social/gendered) valuations of speech and writing are different for male and female adolescents. In the peer-groups of the young man, the (working-class) values attaching to speech are higher than those attaching to writing: whole clusterings of values around masculinity, identification with (oppositional) sub-groupings (in relation to school, for instance), may make the male writer uncomfortable with (too great an identification with, especially) the syntax of written language. That unease appears predominantly in the speech-like clausal syntax of the sentence forms used by him. Examples are the first two sentences: the two clauses in the first sentence are weakly integrated, for writing; so are the first clause and the second (main) clause in the second sentence. Both sentences are perfectly fine when spoken, that is, when the integrating resources of intonation provide appropriate linking. To turn each of the two sentences into 'proper' sentences very little needs to be done. A semi-colon would mark an adequate writing-like relation; so would a conjunction such as 'because'. A broad constellation of sets of social values means that working-class forms of communication, speech in particular, are associated with, and in part express, complex sets of values of masculinity. This makes it hard, or even impossible, for this young male writer to adopt and to produce for himself the full representational resources of written language. The kinds of subjectivity which are associated with 'writing' and produced by these are not what he wants to be, or to develop. However, this is only one part of the story. His competence in the technicist aspects of economics discourse – the technical terminology – is, if anything, greater than that of the young woman writer.

The situation for the young woman may be different. It may be that in her peer-group there are no value systems that are resistant to the production of the syntactic-grammatical forms of writing, and of their broader valuation. To the contrary, in her case there may be value systems which are supportive of these. She produces for herself the full representational resources of the syntax of written language, in this instance in the school subject Economics. With the production of these resources goes the production of a particular subjectivity: a complex of the conceptual/cognitive possibilities of writing and of the social values of writing. In a sense, the grade is a reward for *that* at least as much as for her competence in Economics. An analysis of her text reveals a fine, nuanced attention to interpersonal aspects of the social situation of writing, and a finely nuanced attention to modal discriminations in her argument. To give just an indication. The first two paragraphs are 'formal' in tone, until the introduction in the last sentence, of 'we'. This personalising touch is confirmed in the use of 'you' in the second sentence of the third paragraph; and it is intensified in the less formal 'the poor', 'the rich', and the ' "got it in the neck" ', nicely distanced through the use of scare quotes. There are other indicators; the effect, however, is an address to the reader both formal and familiar; conveying an ease with the subject matter, and a confidently established position for the writer. Consider, for instance, her use of 'we' at the end of the second paragraph – after she has established a securely 'objective' tone; or the use of 'you' at the start of the third paragraph: both uses prepare the way for the increasingly informal tone – closely controlled – 'left better off', 'didn't', and the distanced yet informal ' "got it in the neck" '; etc. These devices establish a precisely articulated position for herself *vis-a-vis* her readers. It may be that these characteristics too, have 'feminine' valuations in her cultural group and society.

There are other considerations which I have not developed in my argument here. In general my account assumes a view of language as a dynamic rather than as a stable or even a static system. That in itself, especially the transmission of either view in curricula as in pedagogies, has effects on the production of subjectivity – supporting attitudes towards authority, as against developing ideas of individual agency, for instance. The question, always puzzling to me, of the development of the personality of the 'working-class Tory', may rest as much in the modes of teaching of punctuation, of reading, and of writing, as in other more likely candidates. One large consequence of my approach is its implication for the construction of curricula and for the development of pedagogies. If my position is, broadly speaking, plausible, curricula and their contents, as much as the forms of pedagogies, are designs for subjectivities. This moves the whole debate from the 'now' to the future, from questions of skills to questions of subjectivity, citizenship and forms of society.

4 Changing agendas

And so to conclude.

Four points might serve to map out the terrain for the new debate. The first is that of the dimensions of the context in which the futures of English need to be debated: multiculturalism, polyculturalism; globalisation of culture, of the economy – whether of finance or of production; the changing landscape of communication in the public domain – the shift to the visual, to sound, but also to the body as an expressive, representational, and communicational medium (whether as Rambo, or as American Gladiator, as a WWF star, as jogging or as aerobics).

The second is the reassertion of the centrality of English in any attempt to make the paths towards a culture of innovation, towards working futures. The furious debate over the last seven or eight years over English has demonstrated its intense significance, and yet has left it exhausted of real meaning. Squabbles over apostrophes or texts to be studied; short-term concerns over handwriting or spelling; misconceived notions about writing or reading are, deeply, missing the point. English is central because it represents that subject in the curriculum which, along with Mathematics and Science, puts forward foundational categories for thinking. It goes beyond the latter two in providing us with the means of making our representations of who we are, the means of *seeing ourselves as the makers of our means of making meaning,* and through this, giving children the possibility of seeing themselves as the makers of their futures.

My third point concerns the question just raised: what is the curriculum? What is it *for*? Who is it for? What can, should, must it be and do? Whose interests and whose benefit are to carry the day? My answer may be uncomfortably interventionist: however, I am clear that inaction is as potent a form of action as action itself; and to put issues out on the table at least enables everyone who ought to participate in a discussion to do so. English is or can become, must become in my view, one central means of participating in making the future which we wish to see.

Lastly, there is the question of curriculum and its contents. I put forward the idea that content needs to be rethought in the most serious fashion. Ideas of content are being remade before our very eyes, without anyone actually realising this, seemingly. From the *production and dissemination of knowledge*, which was, over the last two centuries, the underpinning metaphor, education is being wrenched in the new direction of the *deployment and management of information*. The latter is essential, I am certain; the production of knowledge will remain essential also. The idea that we now have all the knowledge we need rests on a deep misunderstanding of the dynamic interaction of social practice and theory, a misunderstanding of the historicity of knowledge.

Unless we are envisaging, literally, the end-of-civilisation-as-we-know-it, there is a continuing need for the making of new understandings. That sense of what education is has to reach right down into primary schools, and certainly needs to be central in the curricula of the secondary school. English is the subject which is responsible for providing us with the means of making our visions, and so this must be a guiding element in our thinking about its curriculum.

Throughout this book I have stressed the importance of difference as the major resource in culturally and economically productive futures. I have spoken of the need to engender a disposition which moves well beyond mere 'tolerance': tolerance acknowledges and accepts difference, but does not turn it into a productive resource. It remains for me to stress commonality. I take it as an absolute given that there is a 'we' in this place 'England', and perhaps in this entity called Britain, who feel that it is only if we act in commonality that there is a future which is in any sense a positive one. So my arguments around difference are founded on the assumptions of shared goals by all groups in 'England', not in an attempt to flatten out differences, but in a real attempt to construct a frame of overarching aims, within which all the groups present here can achieve their legitimate goals. That presupposes mutual support, and co-operation, as the only available means of achieving productive futures.

Acknowledgement of and respect *for* difference does not rule out the recognition of that overarching set of aims. In that newer conception of equity which I mentioned earlier, respect for difference is not only the respect of majority groups for the values of the minority, but also an acknowledgement of and respect for the values of the majority. This will be contentious for some readers. But histories are important and cannot be set aside without the production of conflict and tension. The assertion of an aim of dignity for all is just that: dignity for all.

Agendas are changing. The syntax of that clause suggests an event without causation, or a causation of a cosmic kind, a 'natural' event, akin to 'sea-levels are rising'. We think we know that we may have something to do with the rising of sea-levels. Agendas are changing because agendas are being changed: others, about whose commitment to social responsibility I have the severest misgivings, have an absolute confidence about their right to set their agendas for us. The traditional role of the academic, of offering critique, seems to me now akin to the efforts of King Canute: worse, I think it amounts to an embarrassed turning away from the increasingly savage realities of social life. That has happened before in this century on this continent. I think that we, all of us, have more than a right, we have a responsibility to take our part in making the future as we think it ought to be made.

Bibliography

Books mentioned or invoked in the text:

Bourdieu, P. (1990) (ed. Thompson, J.) *Language and Symbolic Power.* Cambridge: Polity Press

Cope, B. and Kalantzis, M. (eds) (1993) *The Powers of Literacy: A Genre Approach to Teaching Writing.* Lewes: Falmer Press

Gee, J.P. (1994) *New Alignments and Old Literacies: Critical Literacy, Post-modernism, and Fast Capitalism.* Worcester, Mass: Hiatt Centre

Halliday, M.A.K. (1985) *Introduction to Functional Grammar.* London: Edward Arnold

Hutton, W. (1995) *The State We're In.* London: Jonathan Cape

Peters, T. (1992) *Literation Management: Necessary Disorganization for the Nanosecond Nineties.* New York: Faucett

Peters, T. (1994) *The Tom Peters Seminar: Crazy Times Call for Crazy Organizations.* New York: Vintage Books

Saussure, F. (1974) tr. Baskin, W. *Course in General Linguistics.* Glasgow: Collins

Senge, P.M. (1991) *The Fifth Discipline: The Art and Practice of the Learning Organization.* New York: Doubleday

Some readers may wish to know where I 'come from' intellectually and politically. I therefore list some books which will provide an indication. I list them in the order in which they were first written.

Kress, G.R. (ed.) (1976) *Halliday: System and Function in Language.* Oxford: Oxford University Press

Hodge, R.I.V. and Kress, G.R. (1993) *Language as Ideology.* (2nd edition) London: Routledge

Aers, D.R., Hodge, R.I.V., and Kress, G.R. (1982) *Literature, Language and Society in England 1580–1680.* Dublin: Gill and Macmillan

Kress, G.R. (1994) *Learning to Write.* (2nd edition) London: Routledge

Kress, G.R. (1989) *Linguistic Processes in Sociocultural Practice.* Oxford: Oxford University Press

Hodge, R.I.V. and Kress, G.R. (1988) *Social Semiotics.* Cambridge: Polity Press

Kress, G.R. and van Leeuwen, T. (1995) *Reading Images: The Grammar of Visual Design.* London: Routledge

Note: I wish to thank Andrew Lambirth for his permission to use Olayinka's image of the queen from Snow White on page 73. Without knowing him I would like to thank the young maker of that image. Thanks also to Christina Tsai and her daughter Sarah; and to Michael and Emily Kress; for allowing me to use their materials.